We all want to live life to the fullest, regardless of the time that lies ahead. Strangely, by understanding and accepting death we are freed to live, whether we're healthy or ill, young or old.

Joseph Bayly has written a book of rare sensitivity and frankness about the subject that was taboo in our culture until a few years ago.

What is dying like? How can we cope with overwhelming grief? What does serious illness do to a family? What if the dying one is a child? Is there life after death? How can we be sure?

The author, who has lost three sons of his own, offers insight and practical help. He has held seminars on the subject (some in association with Dr. Elisabeth Kübler-Ross) for doctors and nurses, hospital chaplains and pastors, and for students in colleges and universities.

> *"Bayly writes as a very sensitive human being . . . a gift to those in grief."*
> Christian Medical Society Journal

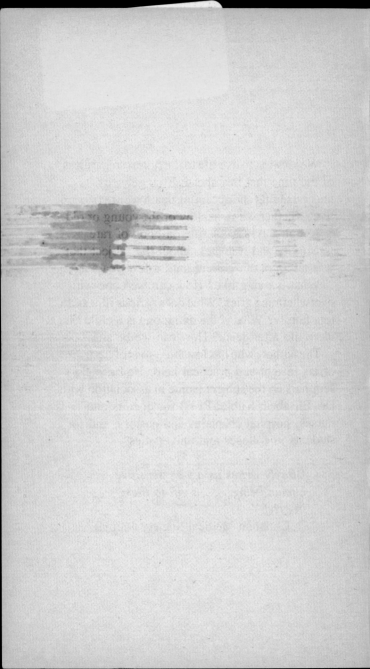

JOSEPH BAYLY

The Last Thing We Talk About

David C. Cook Publishing Co.

ELGIN, ILLINOIS—WESTON, ONTARIO

Formerly published as
THE VIEW FROM A HEARSE

First Printing, June 1969

90 89 88 87 86 20 19 18

© 1969 David C. Cook Publishing Co., Elgin, IL 60120
© 1973 David C. Cook Publishing Co., Elgin, IL 60120 Revised Edition

Printed in the United States of America
Library of Congress Catalog Card Number 70-87318
ISBN: 0-912692-07-3

Cover Design by Kurt Dietsch

To the memory
of three sons
Danny, John and Joe
who introduced us
to death
—its tragedy, its glory

Contents

All mankinde is of one Author, and is one volume; when one Man dies, one Chapter is not torne out of the booke, but translated into a better language; and every Chapter must be so translated. God emploies several translators: some peeces are translated by age, some by sicknesse, some by warre, some by justice; but Gods hand is in every translation; and his hand shall binde up all our scattered leaves againe, for that Librarie where every booke shall lie open to one another.

— JOHN DONNE (1573-1631)

1. The Predictable Event

THE HEARSE began its grievous journey many thousand years ago, as a litter made of saplings.

Litter, sled, wagon, Cadillac: the conveyance has changed, but the corpse it carries is the same.

Birth and death enclose man in a sort of parenthesis of the present. And the brackets at the beginning and end of life are still impenetrable.

This frustrates us, especially in a time of scientific breakthrough and exploding knowledge, that we should be able to break out of earth's environment and yet be stopped cold by death's unyielding mystery. Electroencephalogram may replace mirror held before the mouth, autopsies may become more sophisticated, cosmetic embalming may take the place of pennies on the eyelids and canvas shrouds, but death continues to confront us with its blank wall. Everything changes; death is changeless.

We may postpone it, we may tame its violence, but death is still there waiting for us.

Death always waits. The door of the hearse is never closed.

Dairy farmer and sales executive live in death's shadow, with Nobel prize winner and prostitute, mother, infant, teen, old man. The hearse stands

11

waiting for the surgeon who transplants a heart as well as the hopeful recipient, for the funeral director as well as the corpse he manipulates.

Death spares none.

The certainty of death, and of participation with all mankind in this terminal event, might be a source of individual security. But it is not. It is rather the focus of man's insecurity and fear, his inability to be completely sure of anything on earth because he cannot be sure of drawing his next breath, or the one after.

What is death?

A few years ago I was waiting to see Dr. Irving Wolman, hematologist at Philadelphia Children's Hospital. The day before, we had buried our almost-five-year-old, who had died of leukemia. Now I was waiting to thank the man who had been so kind to our little boy and to us during the nine months between diagnosis and death.

Dr. Wolman's secretary beckoned to me. When I approached her desk, she did not tell me, as I expected, that the doctor would now see me. Instead, she looked toward a little boy playing on the floor. In my preoccupation I had failed to notice any others in the waiting room.

"He has the same problem your little boy had." The secretary spoke quietly.

I sat down next to the little boy's mother. We were far enough away from him, and we talked softly enough, that he could not hear us.

"It's hard bringing him in here every two weeks for these tests, isn't it." I didn't ask a question; I stated a fact. The uncertainty whether a child is

12

still in remission, or the fearful cells will reappear under the microscope, makes the mind run wild.

"Hard?" She was silent for a moment. "I die every time. And now he's beginning to sense that something's wrong . . ." Her voice trailed off.

"It's good to know, isn't it," I spoke slowly, choosing my words with unusual care, "that even though the medical outlook is hopeless, we can have hope for our children in such a situation. We can be sure that after our child dies, he'll be completely removed from sickness and suffering and everything like that, and be completely well and happy."

"If I could only believe that," the woman replied. "But I don't. When he dies, I'll just have to cover him up with dirt and forget I ever had him." She turned back to watching her little boy push a toy auto on the floor.

"I'm glad I don't feel that way." I didn't want to say it, I wanted to leave her alone with her apprehension, I wanted to be alone with my grief. But I was compelled to speak—perhaps with the same compulsion I feel to write this book.

"Why?" This time she didn't turn toward me, but kept watching her child.

"Because we covered our little boy up with dirt yesterday afternoon. I'm in here to thank Dr. Wolman for his kindness today."

"You look like a rational person." (I was glad she didn't say, "I'm sorry.") She was looking straight at me now. "How can you possibly believe that the death of a man, or a little boy, is any different from the death of an animal?"

13

2. Death's True Colors

EACH SPRING the road that goes north from our home in Illinois has a succession of animals that have been struck by automobiles. You pass dog, cat, muskrat and mole, as well as masses of unrecognizable fur, flesh and gore, all cold and motionless.

Yesterday a bird struck the windshield of my car as I was driving at high speed. The flash of blue hit with a sound I hear now, and then was tossed aside.

I felt pity for the bird, as I have felt pity for dead animals on the road: one moment graceful, beautiful, flying, singing, scurrying, burrowing; the next moment dead.

There is something unnatural and grotesque, even wrong, about death.

I think that if we were only confronted with the death of animals, if human beings never died, we would still have a problem. Perhaps it would not be moral (although a ton of metal, under my control, against an ounce or two of bird would seem to involve morality), but it would certainly be an aesthetic problem.

Death destroys beauty.

14

Violent death creates obscenity—tasteless, horrid, raw.

We cannot beautify death. We may live with it and accept it, but we cannot change its foul nature.

The Apostle Paul spoke of death as an enemy, "the last enemy to be destroyed." Death is the enemy of God, of man made in God's image, of animal with which man shares flesh, blood, nerve endings.

When the automobile's victim is human, when a child not a bird, a man not a mole lies dead on the road, we see the true nature of death, the dimension of the problem.

We see death's colors when an ounce of metal explodes in Robert F. Kennedy's brain, in Martin Luther King, Jr.'s neck. Images of the dying leaders etch our memory core beyond smashed bird or crushed animal, infinitely beyond, as human potential is terminated so suddenly, so terribly, so early.

Beauty destroyed by ten pills, achievement terminated by a seven-story fall, youth's glory ended by a grenade, women and children charred by napalm: these are the faces of death.

Coronary, cancer, stroke, infection. Death comes, even normally, in a multitude of ways, to every human condition, every age.

Shall we deny death and try to make it beautiful?

A corpse is never beautiful, animal corpse or corpse of man.

Death is an offense to beauty; no embalmer's art can possibly restore it.

We may soften the horror of death by honoring

the corpse. We may patch it up, preserve it, dress it in going-away clothes, place it on a restful couch, surround it with flowers, arrange the pink, pale lights, burn it or bury it.

But disposing of the body does not provide a satisfying answer to the mystery of death, at least for most people.

Nor for humanity's thinkers, who have pondered the subject since the beginning. Socrates held that the essence of philosophy is preparation for death; so does Karl Jaspers two millennia later.

Before Socrates, the Old Testament book of Job described death as "the king of terrors." King David put it bluntly: "The terrors of death have fallen upon me. Fear and trembling come upon me, and horror overwhelms me."

Death's horror is universal.

Surprisingly, one of the two events common to every human being's existence has been considered unnatural by every generation of man, including our own.

What is it about death that creates this unnatural horror in us?

For one thing, death is the supreme enigma. We cannot explain its mystery and the unknown makes us fear. This mystery is greatest in a generation whose stance toward death is denial.

Another element of death that is unnatural, and makes us dread, is the pain that frequently accompanies dying. Pain may be extended over a long period of time, or it may be sudden and overwhelming. But it's a part of death.

Then there's the termination of every human relationship. This termination may be quite abrupt, providing no opportunity to set affairs in order. Death is the great interrupter.

Decomposition of the body is another element of death that contributes to our sense of dread. We spend a lifetime caring for our bodies; it is hardly pleasant to contemplate a time when they will return to dust.

In spite of death's endless repetition, it is still not natural. Nor will it ever be.

3. To Face Death

WE ARE CRITICAL of the Victorians because they sentimentalized death and surrounded it with pathos.

But modern man denies it. The sort of taboo Victorians placed on public discussion of sex has been transferred to death in our culture.

When death is seriously presented (as in the Theater of the Absurd), it is ridiculed as a cosmic joke, or defined as a meaningless accident in a meaningless universe.

This conspiracy of silence in the twilight of the century has produced a denial of death without precedent in Western civilization. And it has its effects.

Perhaps the most significant is failure to come to grips with life. From the beginning of time, philosophers have pinpointed confrontal with death as the key to life. If we would understand life, they say, we must grapple with death's mystery, search for its meaning, come to terms with its nature.

The Psalmist expressed this thought in a variety of ways: "Lord, let me know my end, and what is the measure of my days; let me know how fleeting my life is. Behold, thou hast made my days a few handbreadths, and my lifetime is as nothing in

18

thy sight. Surely every man goes about as a shadow. Surely for nought are they in turmoil; man heaps up, and knows not who will gather. . . . So teach us to number our days that we may get a heart of wisdom." (Revised Standard Version)

Exposure to death does something of great value to us. "The question of the meaning and worth of life never becomes more urgent or more agonizing than when we see the final breath leave a body which a moment before was living." (Carl Jung)

Unfortunately (from the standpoint of gaining this personal insight) death is not a frequent incident in contemporary America. One estimate is that the average person may go through a twenty-year period without being exposed to death in his immediate family or circle. And when death does come, medical personnel are often the only ones present to see the final breath leave the body.

The combination of cultural death-denial and absence of opportunity to observe the death event produces heightened fear of death in many people.

We fear what we don't understand.

Most of us keep our feeling about death to ourselves. In so doing we find, not surprisingly, that the subject can more easily be excluded from conversation and discussion than from our inner thought. And when we think about it, we fear it to a certain extent.

Some who are almost totally ignorant of death's meaning fear it the most, and fit a New Testament description most closely: "Through fear of death [they are] subject to lifelong bondage."

Martin Heidegger, German philosopher, says

that "death is something which nobody can do for another." And an understanding of death is something nobody can achieve for another. We must grapple with it, conquer it ourselves.

A few people face death with expectancy. It is the Great Adventure, beside which moon landings and space trips pale in significance.

The paradox is that when you accept the fact of death, you are freed to live.

But accepting the fact of death, finding its meaning, facing it squarely: this is not the same as becoming obsessed with it.

In La Rochefoucauld's words, "One can no more look steadily at death than at the sun."

Gertrude Stein is said to have told Ernest Hemingway that he ceased to be a great writer when he became obsessed with sex and death.

The contemporary denial of death also makes it difficult for us to empathize with the terminally ill person and, after his death, with his survivors. Comfort is a lost art, except for choosing a greeting card. (Our ambivalent feelings about death are reflected here, even: the manufacturers have not yet produced personalized sympathy cards for a favorite nephew, a sister-in-law, or a dear aunt.)

I think another effect of our denial of death is renewed interest in communication with the dead.

If this is fraud on the part of spiritualists and mediums, the opportunity comes in a death-denying society through vulnerability caused by grief. If it is real communication, historical precedent (including King Saul's conversation with the prophet Samuel through the Witch of Endor) indicates that this occurs in times of spiritual darkness rather than light.

When a civilization denies death, and hems its members in with cars and amusements, science and organ transplants, against the mystical elements of life that reach their zenith in death, we should not be surprised if young men and women create their own mystery through consciousness-expanding drugs and Eastern religions. Nor, perhaps, should we be surprised if that civilization has a high rate of mental illness and suicide.

4. Styles of Dying Change

DEATH overtakes us in a multitude of ways.

Disease heads the list, although the last century has seen the taming of many past killers. Typhus, typhoid, smallpox and diphtheria are among those that no longer claim their quota of lives, at least in countries with modern medical technology.

On the other hand, diseases related to aging have increased. So have those that arise out of problem areas of modern life: pollution, stress, diet and lethargy.

Accidental death has also increased. The era of machinery and rapid transit has been accompanied by acceleration in the incidence of this kind of death.

Perhaps the outstanding death innovation of our times is mass killing. Bombing of cities in World War II, which culminated in the atomic destruction of Nagasaki and Hiroshima, introduced a new form of death. The hydrogen bomb has caused the whole civilized world to sit in the shadow of sudden destruction. Death is our "constant companion."

Genocide is another form of mass death, revived in our generation. Adolf Hitler's extermination of six million Jews is at once something new and something old.

In recent years, acts of violence that produce death have increased in our American society. The ready availability of the gun that insulates a killer against personal contact with those he kills—feeling their flesh—and provides a coward's advantage, is a considerable factor in this increase.

But death is death, whether by cancer in ancient Egypt or in New York's Memorial Hospital; whether by cross or noose or gas chamber or electric chair; by knife or gun; by stone catapult or rocket; by starvation in a besieged city or obliterating hydrogen bomb.

Mass death produces monumental problems for survivors, but it does not change the nature of death for those who die.

Is death pure chance, a random happening that overtakes an individual?

Many people find a bit of reassurance in high-risk situations by such a statement as, "When my number comes up I'll die, but not before."

The Bible seems to support this attitude toward death, but with certain limitations. God reserved to Himself power over Job's life, and Job explained that man's "days are determined, and the number of his months is with thee, and thou hast appointed his bounds that he cannot pass."

God is the one who determines when we shall die, according to the Bible. King David prayed that God would not take him away in the midst of his days. Jesus Christ "knew that his hour had come to depart out of this world to the Father." God extended the life of the Old Testament King Hezekiah fifteen years when he turned to God in repentance.

23

In that mysterious relationship between God's sovereignty and man's freedom, the length of life may be affected by our own actions. Several acts of suicide are recorded in the Bible. St. Paul spoke of those who partook of the Lord's Supper unworthily as dying prematurely.

On one occasion I was present when a group of medical doctors discussed the termination of life. One outstanding doctor expressed his own opinion in these words, as I recall them: "I am convinced that God decides the issues of life and death. One patient dies, another recovers, from what seem to be very similar situations. I knew a doctor once who administered a several-times-lethal dose of morphine to a severely damaged infant and the infant did not die. I think God did not want it to die."

The assurance that God controls the issues of life and death brings confidence in crisis periods.

Shortly after our five-year-old died of leukemia, someone asked me how I'd feel if a cure for leukemia were then discovered. My answer was that I'd be thankful, but it would be irrelevant to the death of my son. God determined to take him to His home at the age of five; the means was incidental.

5. What Is Dying Like?

DEATH is the permanent, irreversible cessation of vital functions of the body.

Not all functions stop at the same time. Until recently, the lack of heartbeat was considered final evidence of death.

Now the medical criterion for determining when death has occurred is being re-examined, partly because of the desire for organs from just-dead bodies for transplant surgery. Another reason the new guidelines are needed is that modern respirators, heart stimulators and other supportive measures sometimes can keep a patient breathing and his heart beating for long periods of time, even when his brain has no possibility of ever functioning again.

So attention has shifted from heart to brain for a reliable criterion of when death has occurred. The electroencephalogram (EEG) provides this: a flat EEG indicates that no brain waves are being produced. Therefore the brain, control center of the body and center of personhood, is dead. (Measurement of oxygen flow to the brain to find whether it has ceased may make this criterion even more definitive.)

Death is the one certainty of life. "We begin to

die as soon as we are born," according to Voltaire.

What is dying like?

For the elderly person, it may be the quiet culmination of the aging of vital organs. Often there is no pain, even in those who die of malignancies, for old age frequently brings alleviation of symptoms and blunting of sensibility.

Recent research indicates that the elderly do not usually have increased fear of dying, unless they are in a state of environmental stress brought on primarily by being about to be moved into homes for the aged.

Death may be a relatively quiet and peaceful transition at other ages as well, particularly if it follows a debilitating disease.

But often it is not, especially among the young who have responsibilities which they must leave behind, unfinished, for others. The knowledge that death impends may produce emotional as well as physical distress.

Dr. Cicely Saunders, of London's St. Joseph's Hospice, which cares almost exclusively for the incurably ill, says that this is the time people can be emotionally and psychologically most mature.

"You remember when Pope John said, 'My bags are packed. I am ready to leave.' We are helping patients to pack their bags—each in his own individual way and making his own choices."

The greatest need in these cases, Dr. Saunders says, is for a sympathetic listener who will devote time to the case. She once asked a patient who knew that he was dying what he wanted to see in people who were looking after him.

His answer: "For someone to look as if they are trying to understand me."

Is there such a thing as "the art of dying"?

Yes, says British surgeon and gynecologist John Beattie. "The ideal surely is the passing of the spirit from the body under sublime and peaceful circumstances. Also, this is seen at its best when a patient is filled with 'the peace of God, which passeth all understanding.' I suppose that we have all witnessed such a death from time to time.

"The best example in my own experience was that of a young woman dying of a malignant ovarian tumor. It might have been expected that she would have had great pain and discomfort from massive ascites and a peritoneal cavity filled with growth, yet she was completely at peace, although knowing clearly that there was no hope of prolongation of life. She looked forward to meeting her Lord Jesus Christ. She also had no anxiety at all for her husband who was to be left behind, for she had absolute faith that he would be cared for and would in due course join her.

"An atheist of my acquaintance would just label this condition 'euphoria.' So it is, but it is not due to drugs, nor to semi-consciousness, but to the power of God Himself. We may ask ourselves why we so seldom see a person dying with such positive support and with so much peace and assurance." (*The Doctor, the Patient and the Art of Dying*, London, Christian Medical Fellowship.)

I think that some religious people, with the very best intentions, have idealized the actual moment of dying to the extent that relatives and friends faced with the reality are unprepared.

They have done this with deathbed stories, visions of beauty that overtook the dying person, and accounts of significant last words.

Doubtless these things occasionally happen, at least when the dying person is elderly. But death is a terrible enemy, and even for one with faith in God, the enemy has not yet been destroyed.

So a struggle to live, heartbreaking convulsions, and crying out with physical needs instead of nice little "last words" should not surprise us if we are exposed to a person in the act of dying.

6. People Used to Die at Home

ONE of my early memories is of being led into my grandmother's room in Gettysburg, Pennsylvania, to give her a final kiss. She was dying, I had been told, "so be quiet and behave."

That scene impresses me today with its Old Testament quality. Grandma, an imposing person, was conscious, slightly raised on a bolster, her white hair braided and carefully arranged on the quilt she had made as a young woman. The bed, a four-poster, was the one in which she had slept for fifty years, in which her four children had been conceived and born.

The wide-boarded floor creaked its familiar creak, the kerosene lamp flickered on the massive bureau, a bouquet of sweet peas from Grandma's garden made the room faintly fragrant.

The old lady was surrounded by her children and grandchildren. In a few hours she died.

Forty years later my children were with their grandfather when he had his last heart attack. We gave him oxygen, called the doctor, and then the ambulance came. The men put Grandpa on a stretcher, carried him out of the house, and that was the last his grandchildren saw of him. Children are excluded from most hospitals.

In the intensive care unit of the hospital, my wife and I were with him until the visiting hours were over. The mechanics of survival—tubes, needles, oxygen system, electronic pacemaker—were in him and on him and around him.

Grandpa died alone, at night, after visiting hours. His grandsons had no chance to give him a final kiss, to feel the pressure of his hand on their heads.

In this generation death has moved out of the home to the hospital, doctors and nurses have replaced the family, a dying father has become a terminal patient. If the end seems imminent and the family members are present, they are usually hustled out of the room. Why? To shield them from death's shock, to give medical personnel a free hand if any extreme measures are necessary, perhaps to avoid a traumatic experience for other patients if a surviving relative should go to pieces.

All of this makes sense.

And it creates problems.

The ordinary, age-old fear of death has an added dimension today: the anticipation of being alone in life's closing hour, isolated from those with whom the other hours and years and decades of life have been shared. We have consented to death's banishment from our homes to the hospital, where it is acted out in a setting of sterile equipment and efficient, unfamiliar people.

If it is possible, the ultimate loneliness of dying has become more lonely today. This is the price tag attached to medical advances that have calmed some of death's agonies, deadened some of its pain, prolonged the process of dying.

But advanced medical technology and better nursing care are not the only reasons we send people to the hospital to die. One authority says that eighty percent of Americans today die in institutions, including hospitals, homes for the aged and similar facilities. Many of these persons could die as well, perhaps better, at home—if their families were willing to enter into the final days or hours of care. The hospital relieves the family of this responsibility; it does not improve the medical situation.

Dr. Elisabeth Kübler-Ross, authority on death and dying, says that, whenever possible, we should try to arrange for members of our families to die at home. This would, in her opinion, be one of the most helpful changes in the American way of dying.

Obviously it is not always possible, and the attending physician is the one who can best assess and advise in a particular situation. Don't hesitate to discuss the matter with your doctor. Hopefully, he will consider the strength or weakness of the one primarily responsible for the care at home.

Even where there is a sincere desire to keep a person in terminal illness at home, it may not be possible because of work responsibilities outside the home that remove the person who would provide the primary care. If such a situation, or a medical factor—such as the control of pain—makes it necessary for the one we love to be hospitalized for his last days, we should feel no guilt. God knows all the factors in the total situation, and He understands. So, usually, does the person who is dying. And if he doesn't, love may have to show itself by sitting quietly in the presence of criticism or complaint,

31

knowing that if the sick one were well, he would understand.

But the removal of dying people from the familiar home to the hospital is not the only negative result of advances in medical technology. Another price we pay is the loss of dignity in dying.

Perhaps there is a contradiction of terms here; perhaps dying never was, never can be dignified. Yet the indignity is increased by catheters and bottles, electronic devices and all the other paraphernalia of medical extremity.

On one occasion, I was with a woman who was in terminal cancer. Her husband had left the hospital room to call home, to make sure the young children were all right.

Suddenly she stopped breathing. I called the nurse, an older woman, who came at once and found the pulse was stilled. She called for an intern, and while we waited, closed her eyes and murmured a prayer: "Please Lord, no heroics."

Possibly another week or month of life is worth it. The possibility of extending life even longer may make extreme measures necessary to fulfill the physician's Hippocratic oath.

The decision to interrupt and delay death by heroic measures, or by breathing machines, intravenous feeding, or various other means, is completely in the hands of the attending physician. And it is one of the greatest burdens a conscientious person can bear.

We must try to understand the physician's responsibility and decision, believing that he is motivated by what he perceives to be the best interest of the patient. Occasionally the doctor may share his responsibility by discussing the alternatives with a close relative of the dying person. Many doctors, however, feel that the stress of the situation precludes clear judgment and may possibly open the door to depression and guilt at a later date. So they keep their own counsel.

The possibility of a suit for malpractice is often in the background of a medical doctor's decisions, including the one to prolong life by every possible means, even though the person may have irreversible brain damage.

I believe the question, "What would you think was best if this were your own mother (father, child)?" is an appropriate one to ask a doctor if extraordinary measures to prolong life for a strictly limited period of time are being discussed.

A few years ago a friend of mine, a godly man who had responded with courage and acceptance to the burden of cancer for many months, was in the hospital, weak and dying. His doctor had told him and his wife that he could not live longer than a week or two. One Sunday night, after a beautiful final visit with his wife, alone after her departure, my friend pulled the needle that was sustaining his life from his arm, shut off the valve, rolled up the tube and went to sleep. The next day he died.

Did he take his own life? No, I believe not. What he did was merely to remove the means by which the doctor could delay his death for a few days, prolonging the suffering of his wife, delaying his soul's flight to God.

Our little boy died at home. He began to bleed

at six o'clock in the morning. The doctor came a little later and said, "I could put him in the hospital and he could have a massive transfusion. Maybe he'd live a few days longer, maybe not."

We chose to have him stay at home, in the familiar bedroom, with his father and mother to comfort him and love him and talk to him about Jesus' love and heaven.

In the previous months, when we knew that he had leukemia—and even before—we had talked naturally about these things, and he had responded with the simple faith of a child in what his parents tell him.

Now he didn't want to go to heaven. He wanted to stay with us in the familiar home. (What little boy wants to leave his mother and daddy, his brothers and his sister?)

At two-thirty in the afternoon, he died.

Died?

In Jesus' words, "the angels carried him" to heaven.

7. Understanding the Dying Person

ALL OF US—doctor or nurse, family or friend—
want to provide all the support we can to the person
who is going to die. But we're often at a loss over
what to say, what to do.

To be freed up so that we can help, we have to
understand the dying person's feelings, and our
own.

The first thing we should realize is that he probably knows he is going to die, whether he's been
told or not. Dr. Thomas P. Hackett, chief of psychiatric consultation service at Massachusetts General Hospital in Boston, says that observations pooled
from many investigators working independently in
various parts of the world confirm this. Dr. Elisabeth
Kübler-Ross says that all dying persons know they
are going to die. (Those who die suddenly, usually
accidentally, are of course excepted.)

How does he know if he hasn't been told? Sometimes by inner indications, physical or psychological; more often by an unconscious betrayal of the
truth by those who care for him, or by his family
and friends. Usually this is expressed non-verbally.

Forced joviality, nervousness, briefer visits by
the doctor and fewer questions, a subtle, almost unconscious change in relationships are some ways.

Nurses have mentioned a pattern of behavior to me: first a wife will kiss her husband on the mouth, then on the cheek, then the forehead, and finally she will blow him a kiss from the door. The change is not lost on him.

Dr. Hackett says that those who know they are going to die fear the process of dying more than death itself.

What feelings disturb the person who knows he is going to die?

There's the realization, almost surely disappointing, that his contribution to life is ending. He has achieved what he will, whether in vocation, or raising children, or forming relationships. For the young, especially, death seems premature, an ugly interference with the goals of life.

At the same time there is a growing understanding of the separation death will bring (the kiss blown from the doorway of the hospital room).

This separation isn't just from members of the family. Others tend to become distant, to move away from former closeness. Dr. Kübler-Ross tells of one patient who said, "I know my doctor can't help me any more. But if he'd just call me on the phone and say, 'Josephine, how do you feel?' "

The same feeling was reflected in the statement a dying woman made to me: "My pastor doesn't come to see me very often. I guess he's too busy."

At the same time as relationships may seem to be coming unglued, there's the fear of "becoming a burden." Serious illness is seen as imposing inconvenience on family and friends, such as the time required to make hospital visits. Prolonged illness may be feared as financially disastrous to survivors.

There are personal fears as well. One is the fear of pain, which is inseparably linked with dying in most people's minds, in spite of medical advances in its control.

Another is the fear of personal indignity, of being subjected to medical procedures, to paraphernalia in the body, or to the loss of parts of the body.

These are real fears, all of them. How can we help the dying person cope with them?

Doctors may help by telling the patient the truth about his condition. According to Dr. Hackett, those people who are told the truth have fewer medical, emotional and psychiatric complications than those from whom the truth has been withheld. For instance, some doctors argue that the patient may commit suicide if he is told the truth. But the incidence of suicide in a dying population is not that much higher than in the general population. And when suicide occurs, it usually does so in cases where pain has gone out of control, or where the patient has no one to whom he can turn for emotional support. The reasons for withholding the truth, according to Dr. Hackett, mainly reflect the doctor's point of view and philosophy rather than what best fits the patient.

I was close to a Naval lieutenant, an Annapolis graduate, who had a brain tumor removed at Philadelphia Naval Hospital. He was a strong young man, a former member of Navy's football team, and a mature Christian. A psychiatrist spent a lot of time trying to convince the neurosurgeon—who feared that he couldn't cope with the truth—that the young man should be told that the tumor was malignant. He finally succeeded, partially at least, and the lieutenant lived a glorious last year. But, as the psychiatrist said to me, the neurosurgeon was "saying something about himself rather than his patient."

Psychologist Herman Feifel, in a California research project, discovered that ninety percent of terminal patients were in favor of being told their condition by their doctor, rather than learning it on their own. But ninety percent of the doctors interviewed believed the patient should not be told. There is, however, a strong movement in medicine today to tell the patient the truth, if there are no psychological contraindications.

It is the patient's right to know the truth, and it is his family's right as well. So the patient can request this information.

But if the patient knows that he is going to die anyway, why should he be told? Most importantly, to open the door to talking about his reactions to the knowledge, and to prevent play-acting with his family.

Now the patient may openly talk about his condition, about his fears and his feelings, and we may listen. But we must be sensitive to what he says, both verbally and nonverbally. Tears, turning the face to the wall, not wanting to talk: each of these says something.

And there is symbolic communication. After hearing Dr. Kübler-Ross speak of this, my wife suddenly remembered how her mother had said to her, less than a year before she died, "Now, Mary, I want you to wear my diamond ring." And she took it off to put it on her daughter's finger.

"No, Mother," my wife protested. "You wear it. I don't want to take it from you now."

Today she would accept it, realizing that her mother knew she would soon die, and wanted to give the symbol of herself as wife and mother to her daughter.

The sensitive person will hear what is being said, regardless of the language that is used.

Dr. Elisabeth Kübler-Ross has given the classic description of the coping patterns of patients who know their diagnosis is terminal. This Swiss-born psychiatrist is a most sensitive person who counseled hundreds of patients and their families in her research into death and dying.

The first stage is denial. Upon hearing the diagnosis, the patient reacts with a shocked "No, not me." It can happen to other people, but not to him. According to Dr. Kübler-Ross, this is a healthy stage, and permits the patient and his family to develop other defenses.

Next comes anger or resentment. "Why me?" is the question asked now. "Why my child?" Blame, directed against the doctor, nurses and God often is a part of this stage. The patient should be accepted, his angry words unjudged.

The third stage is bargaining. "Yes me, but—"

"If You'll just give me five years, I'll . . ." "If You'll keep me alive until my children grow up. . . ." This Dr. Kübler-Ross calls a period of temporary truce.

The fourth stage is depression. Now the patient says, "Yes, me." He has the courage to admit that it is happening to him; this acknowledgment brings depression. Preparatory grief is found during this period, both for the patient and for his family. (The family often goes through all stages, along with the patient.)

Finally comes acceptance, a time of facing death calmly. This is often a difficult time for the family, since the patient tends to withdraw, to be silent. (*On Death and Dying*)

To understand that these stages are normal is to be freed from alarm when they occur. We will not fear that a person is "losing his faith" because he becomes angry or depressed over his condition.

Amy Carmichael once said, "In acceptance lieth peace." And it is most true when the acceptance is of impending death.

What can we do during the unfolding of these successive stages? Dr. Kübler-Ross suggests that the best response is to listen, not to try to "prove" anything to the patient, but to listen.

And at times there will be nothing to listen to; we can only sit with the grieving one, lending support by our simple presence.

8. Responding to the Dying Person

WE MUST not only understand the dying person's reactions; we must understand our own. And this is sometimes even more difficult.

Several months ago I visited a friend, a locomotive engineer ten years younger than I, at Toronto General Hospital. He was terminally ill with heart disease. Two weeks later he died.

As I sat there with his wife, the mother of his three young children, and with his sister, I felt almost guilty. There I was, well and strong, having just come in from the cold street, soon to walk out again, older than he, talking to his wife . . . and he was beyond talking, almost beyond living.

I had to reassure myself, in the face of my feelings, that he was happy to see me—that I did not add to his suffering, but rather was a welcome visitor.

One of the most important affirmations we can give to a dying person is the value of his life, including his family. This is essential when life's goals seem only partially attained, even by the aged.

Dr. Viktor E. Frankl tells of an interview, in the presence of his students, with an eighty-year-old patient, a woman suffering from cancer, who was increasingly depressed.

Frankl: "What do you think of when you look back on your life? Has life been worth living?"

Patient: "Well, Doctor, I must say that I had a good life. Life was nice, indeed. And I must thank the Lord for what it held for me. I went to theaters, I attended concerts, and so forth. You see, Doctor, I went there with the family in whose house I have served for many decades as a maid. In Prague, at first, and afterwards in Vienna. And for the grace of all of these wonderful experiences I am grateful to the Lord."

"I nevertheless felt that she was doubtful in so far as the ultimate meaning of her life as a whole was concerned. . . ." [The woman had had no children.]

Frankl: "You should not forget that, for instance, the greatest philosopher of all times, Immanuel Kant, had no children; would anyone venture to doubt the extraordinary meaningfulness of his life? . . . What counts and matters in life is rather to achieve and accomplish something. And this is precisely what you have done. You have made the best of your suffering. You have become an example for our patients as to the way and manner in which you take your suffering upon yourself. I congratulate you on behalf of this achievement and accomplishment, and I also congratulate your roommates who have the opportunity to watch and witness such an example. . . . (My audience now bursts into a spontaneous applause.) This applause concerns you, Frau Kotek. (She is weeping now.) It concerns your life which

42

has been a great achievement and accomplishment. You may be proud of it, Frau Kotek. And how few people may be proud of their lives . . . I should say, your life is a monument. And no one can remove it from the world."

Patient (regaining her self-control): "What you have said, Professor Frankl, is a consolation. It comforts me. Indeed, I never had an opportunity to hear anything like this. . . ." (Slowly and quietly she leaves the lecture hall.)

"Apparently, she now was reassured. A week later she died, like Job one could say, 'saturated of years.' During the last week of her life, however, she was no longer depressed, but on the contrary, full of faith and pride. Obviously, the interview which we had had together had made her aware that her life was meaningful and that even her suffering had not been in vain. Prior to this, she had admitted to Dr. Gerda Becker, who was in charge of her on the ward, that she felt agonized, and more specifically, ridden by the anxiety that she was useless. The last words however, which she uttered, immediately before her death, were: 'My life is a monument. So Professor Frankl said it, to the whole audience, to all students in the lecture hall. My life was not in vain. . . .'

"We may be justified in assuming that Frau Kotek, like Job, 'went to her grave as the harvest was brought to the granary.' "

Some patients tend to be more open about their feelings with a nurse than with their own families. Recognizing this, leaders in the nursing profession today stress "total patient care," which includes ministering to the psychological and spiritual, as well as physical, needs of patients.

A nurse can be a great help to the patient and his family, if she is professionally capable and a sensitive person. She spends a lot of time with the patient, much more than the doctor—and in many instances, even the family—can spend. Her greatest usefulness will be possible if she is not uptight, but has come to an understanding of the meaning of life, and death, herself.

Feeling increasingly isolated from the world and people, the dying patient often desires a touch from another human being. I was first impressed by this some years ago when I visited a reserved, elderly New Englander in the hospital. He was dying, and he knew it. When I reached under the oxygen tent to shake his hand, he grasped my hand and held on to it the whole time I was in his room. He would never have held another man's hand in any other circumstances.

A nurse friend of mine was caring for a patient, an alcoholic from Chicago's Skid Row, seriously ill, at Cook County Hospital. He commented that a certain doctor was "the best one in the hospital."

The nurse was intrigued by his words, and asked, "Why? What makes him the best?"

"Every time he passes my bed, he tweaks my toe." The doctor treated him like a human being, not like a Skid Row derelict or a "terminal case."

Of course, the struggle between professionalism and compassion is a difficult and continuing one.

Perhaps not surprisingly, in some hospitals cleaning women are the biggest help to dying patients, whom they treat as ordinary human beings, without being uptight.

Another person who is most helpful is the one who himself has cancer or another incurable disease, but who has come to terms with death.

I knew such a woman, Carol Guild. Carol, a beautiful woman, had her first operation for cancer when she was under forty. In the aftermath of that operation, she trusted Jesus Christ, and found the meaning of life, and death.

She was a radiant person, in spite of a progression of operations on her mouth, her eye (which was removed), and her face, over the next eight or nine years.

Carol spent a lot of time visiting patients with incurable diseases, and dying people, in various hospitals in the Chicago area.

On one occasion she was sitting at the bedside of a Negro woman, who had just had surgery for cancer.

"Look at me," the woman said. "All my life I've tried to affirm my dignity, and now this cancer. How can I ever find dignity now?"

"You know," Carol said, "the first time I ever vomited and it came out of my eye socket, I thought I could never achieve dignity again. But then I realized that dignity is found in that direction (pointing up), not in this (pointing out)."

The solution to the problem of dignity, of pain, of unrealized goals, of separation from friends and family, is found in that direction. But we often need to have someone point it out to us.

Why do we find it hard to express our feelings —whether as a grieving person or comforter—in the presence of death? Perhaps it is because we have not learned to respond emotionally in the ordinary circumstances of life, "the life that is so daily."

Grief is grief. The response of a woman who learns that she has a malignancy is not different from that of an unmarried girl who gives up her baby to adoption, a young man or woman who experiences a broken engagement, a middle-aged man who is forced into bankruptcy.

And comfort is comfort. We do not suddenly become sensitive, feeling people when confronted by a dying person or his family. We merely show the degree of emotional maturity we have achieved, the degree to which we have been freed from ourselves.

9. The Management of Grief

DEATH is a wound to the living. Almost all of us were pierced when John F. Kennedy, Martin Luther King, Jr. and Robert F. Kennedy were struck down. ("For the first time in years I cried," wrote our Swarthmore College sophomore son—who died unexpectedly as a result of an accident two months later—"when I saw the pictures in *Time* of President Kennedy's casket being carried down the Capitol steps.")

This reaction to death finds expression and explanation in John Donne's words: "No man is an island, entire of itself; every man is a piece of the continent, a part of the main. If a clod be washed away by the sea, Europe is the less, as well as if a promontory were, as well as if a manor of thy friends or of thine own were. Any man's death diminishes me, because I am involved in mankind. And therefore never send to know for whom the bell tolls; it tolls for thee."

But the bell that tolls for anyone who dies tolls most loudly for one who is part of our own family. That is when the wound is most painful, the grief most unremitting.

Months after our 18-year-old son died, the sight of a boy's arm resting on the sill of a car window up ahead was enough to make me pull over to the side of the road because I could no longer see to drive.

A friend who lost her husband after a few years of marriage told us that when she was riding on a plane with a three-abreast seating arrangement, she suddenly would be moved with fresh grief, if a husband and wife were seated next to her, by the little acts of care and thoughtfulness that the husband performed for his wife. This was years after her own husband had died.

These responses to death are normal, or at least, normal for a person who deeply loved the one who died.

It could be said that any natural response to death is proper and healthy; any unnatural one may delay the healing process and be potentially dangerous.

But what is a natural response?

Grief. Tears. An overwhelming sense of loss. Desire to be alone, or to have social contacts severely restricted.

For some—including the very religious—it may be to question God's wisdom, even His love. When Job, the Old Testament patriarch, lost his children, his possessions and his health, he "cursed the day of his birth. And Job said: Let the day perish wherein I was born, and the night which said, 'A man-child is conceived' . . . because it did not shut the doors of my mother's womb . . . Why did I not die at birth, come forth from the womb and expire?"

Job's wife, mother of the children who died, was

even more direct. "Curse God and die!" she shouted at her husband.

Our contemporary C.S. Lewis, brilliant apologist for the Christian faith, had an equally honest reaction to the wound of death. A bachelor until middle life, Lewis found near-ecstatic happiness and completion in his brief marriage to a woman who died of cancer a few years later.

A Grief Observed is his odyssey of grief, originally published under a pseudonym—perhaps because it seemed so out of character for a man with strong faith, who had been so helpful to others who were confronted by doubts about God and grace.

"O God, God," wrote Mr. Lewis, "why did you take such trouble to force this creature out of its shell if it is now doomed to crawl back—to be sucked back—into it?"

This sort of honesty does not turn God away from us, but brings Him near. And it may hasten the healing process. Being brave, on the other hand, putting up a front, pretending that we have no problem may delay healing.

Guilt is another natural response to death's wound.

All of us hurt the person we love, one way or another: we say sharp words, are inconsiderate and impatient, act selfishly. ("One day I realized," said a doctor, "that I was nicer to the girl who runs the elevator at the hospital than I was to my wife.")

In life we have a chance to straighten things out with, "I'm sorry, please forgive me," with gifts and surprises and special acts of love.

Death closes the door on making amends, opens

the door to a flood of "If only . . ." thoughts.

These thoughts are not necessarily related to major ways in which we hurt the one who died. They may be quite trivial. I remember a nagging feeling of guilt for months because I had procrastinated in framing and mounting a scenic mural in the room of a son who died, and never did get the job done.

Another natural response to death is to idealize the one who died. Obviously this only increases guilt, that we could have behaved as we did toward such a person. (Guilt may even cause us to make the person larger than life-size in our memory.)

Still another normal response to death is found in the way some people feel bound to the one who has died.

"What would she want me to do?" "How can I carry on his work?" These are not unusual reactions to grief.

Exposure to death creates in some a fear of their own death, even a set of symptoms not unlike those of the one who died. (One man I know went through a rough year or two after his wife's death, probably related to his spending the final night in the hospital room with her as she was dying after childbirth.)

Death wounds us, but wounds are meant to heal. And—given time—they will. But we must want to be healed. We cannot be like the child who keeps picking the scab from a cut.

Life must move forward, even though we may have lost the one who was dearest to us, even though meaning seems to have been removed from living.

If we feel guilty, we must find forgiveness. We can't say "I'm sorry" to the one who has died, but we can say it to God. (King David, after he had been accessory to the death of the husband of a woman with whom he had committed adultery, and after the infant son born of that adulterous relationship had died, cried to God for forgiveness in Psalm 51, a classic of penitence: "Against thee, thee only, have I sinned, and done that which is evil in thy sight . . . Create in me a clean heart, O God, and put a new and right spirit within me. Cast me not away from thy presence.")

Of course David had real, objective reasons for his guilt feelings. On the other hand, many people who feel most guilty had been almost completely loving toward the person who died, and have no reason for guilt.

The person who does not experience forgiveness, who continues, after months of acute grief, to be filled with "Why didn't I?" thoughts, "If I could just have it all to do again," "If only," is in a potentially dangerous situation. He should talk to a pastor or religious advisor.

Dr. Eugen Kahn, Baylor medical school authority in psychiatry, suggests that the solution to self-pity is to feel pity for someone else and move in the direction of helping that person.

This sort of emotional investment may be a large part of the healing we need for death's wound. Our thoughts will no longer be on what might have been, nor on visiting a cemetery plot or keeping a room "just as it was the last time he was in it," nor on "what she'd like us to do," nor on our own pains and fears of death. We will be freed from bondage to the past to move in a meaningful forward direction.

We have found it so in our own experience. The death of three children is devastating to a mother, adequate explanation for severe emotional difficulty. From a human standpoint, I attribute my wife's stability to the fact that a succession of needy, hurting people stayed in our home for periods of time after our children's deaths. In ministering to the healing of others, my wife—and I—found healing.

And when the wounds of death begin to heal, most people find that their memory of the one who died is freed from sickbed and casket to recall the person he really was: laughing, frowning, encouraging, working, playing, life-size.

10. How Do You Comfort?

SOME PEOPLE faced with grief escape into fantasy. This is not surprising where personal relationships were strong, and love and life were shared in a multitude of situations for few or many years.

A double bed is suddenly single. A high chair is empty. A table is not set. A telephone is unanswered.

We encourage fantasy-escape from overwhelming loss by much of what we say, much of what is written.

"He is not gone . . . he is in the next room."

But he's not. He's gone and he'll never return. He won't walk through that door again ever, she'll never again have the table set and dinner waiting in the oven, the baby will never spill another glass of milk.

Death is that final.

So if we want to help the sorrowing person, if we want to encourage him to go forward in living that must be radically different, we'll encourage him to grasp reality quite firmly. We won't encourage any flights into fantasy.

We won't deny the reality of death's separation when we talk to a grieving person. If anything, we'll try to strengthen reality in his mind.

Realistic handling of grief probably begins with honest expression of feelings. Tears are valid and helpful for adults as well as children, men as well as women.

Jesus wept at the tomb of a friend, in the presence of his friend's sisters.

Death is never a happy experience. Even when the one who dies has suffered pain for months or years, the memory of pre-suffering life and relationships remains.

We place an intolerable burden on our grieving friends or relatives if we suggest that they try to abstain from tears "for the sake of the children," "because it's not the way a person with your faith should behave," or for some other reason.

Expert opinion seems to be that immediate comprehension and acceptance of the reality of loss and immediate expression of grief are most helpful in recovering from the shock of death's separation and moving forward in life.

For this reason, many physicians do not lessen the force of death's blow to a survivor by prescribing tranquilizers or other emotion- or consciousness-dulling drugs, unless a specific and overriding reason for medication exists.

This is also why viewing the body in its casket is not condemned as a barbaric procedure for survivors. These hours with the corpse before burial prove the finality of death's separation to many people as nothing else could.

Of course we talk to the grieving person. What do we say?

We are most likely to be helpful with an economy of words. In our contacts with people at death as at other times, it is easy to say too much, to talk when we ought to listen.

"When Job's friends came to see him after his children died and he had suffered in so many other ways," suggests a friend of mine who's a psychiatrist, "they missed the opportunity to go down in history as uniquely sensitive and understanding. There they sat on the ground with him for seven days and nights, and they didn't say a word, because they saw how utterly grief-stricken he was. But then they began to talk and spoiled it all."

Sensitivity in the presence of grief should usually make us more silent, more listening.

"I'm sorry," is honest; "I know how you feel," is usually not—even though you may have experienced the death of a person who had the same familial relationship to you as the deceased person had to the grieving one.

If the person feels that you can understand, he'll tell you. Then you may want to share your own honest, not prettied-up feelings in your personal aftermath with death.

Don't try to "prove" anything to a survivor. An arm about the shoulder, a firm grip of the hand, a kiss: these are the proofs grief needs, not logical reasoning.

I was sitting, torn by grief. Someone came and talked to me of God's dealings, of why it happened, of hope beyond the grave. He talked constantly, he said things I knew were true.

I was unmoved, except to wish he'd go away. He finally did.

Another came and sat beside me. He didn't talk. He didn't ask leading questions. He just sat beside me for an hour and more, listened when I said something, answered briefly, prayed simply, left.

I was moved. I was comforted. I hated to see him go.

Many of us move into a house of mourning with our heavy artillery: we spend time, cook food, take care of the children, do the wash, invite out for meals, and in various other ways show our love and protect the survivor from feeling the full blow of his loss.

Others at a distance write letters and send flowers to the grieving person.

This pattern of extreme sensitivity and help continues for a week or so after the funeral, then life catches up with us and we leave the person to feel, belatedly, his extreme loss. And he is now alone.

Immediate help is needed. But even in the first few days it may be better to let the surviving person make some decisions, do some of his own work, face some of the implications and problems, than to do everything for him.

We should not force our will on a grieving person, even when we think we know best. Such decisions as what sort of casket should be chosen, whether and how to dispose of the clothing of the person who has died, should be made with the full agreement of, if not by, the survivor.

An older person needs the dignity of consultation and involvement no less than the young.

The other part of this is that the full force of death and its resulting loss does not strike immediately, especially when the survivor is surrounded by loving, serving friends. If may be weeks or months later when desperate loneliness and grief overwhelm the person.

We should therefore balance immediate with continuing and remote acts of thoughtfulness and love.

For many years—at least fifteen—a Boston doctor sent flowers to a lonely woman on the death anniversary of the woman's mother. The doctor, who happened to be a woman, had attended the mother in her final illness and could sense how desolate the recurring date would be to the daughter, who was then past middle life and a semi-invalid. They had no contact except the flowers, but the flowers said that someone really cared.

As time passes, the sensitive person will remember that for some the grief is not silenced, only muted. This is especially true of parents who have lost children, widows and widowers who have not remarried. Occasionally mentioning the one who died, recalling an incident or happy occasion from the past, usually brings healing rather than pain to the person who still grieves. We are inclined to avoid speaking of the one who died, thinking that to do so would cause fresh grief. But our silence raises questions: Do we really miss the one who died, did the former friendship or relationship ever mean anything to us, is the survivor alone in his sorrow?

Actions as well as words are needed to bring comfort in death's aftermath. Moses in the Old Testament, and Paul in the New, commanded special concern and care for widows.

St. James defined "religion that is pure and undefiled before God" as "visiting orphans and widows in their affliction." Doubtless, women are more able to cope with the affairs of life in our culture than in the first century, and government (through Social Security and other benefits) now provides some financial assistance to widows and orphans. But the need for additional advisory and supportive assistance from friends continues.

The local church or other religious group should provide this sort of continuing reinforcement. We ought to mobilize our resources to bring people who are in darkness and need out into light and self-sufficiency again. "One must help the weak," wrote St. Paul, "remembering the words of the Lord Jesus, how he said, 'It is more blessed to give than to receive.' "

Some teen-agers respond to the shock and grief of death (usually of a parent, but sometimes of a sibling or friend) by becoming anti-social. One study of 14 juvenile delinquents counseled in a Los Angeles precinct revealed that all had gone through a death experience.

Boys who have lost their father, girls who have lost their mother need the influence of a man or woman in their lives during the teen years; so do younger children. Leaders of club activities in the church, camp counselors and other youth workers should be especially alert to these continuing needs. So should neighbors and friends.

Our response to grief should be simple and matched to the need as we see it. An invitation to Sunday dinner, an offer to shovel snow from the walk or prune a tree, including a child who has lost his father on a fishing trip: these are acts that go beyond comfort—although they are comforting—into the area of encouraging a healthy, forward direction in a life that would otherwise be desolate and impoverished.

Time heals grief; love prevents scar tissue from forming.

11. Explaining Death to a Child

DEATH AND SEX have one thing in common: parents are hard put to explain them to children.

We pass on our own hangups, our embarrassment and fears, rather than the reality they will some day have to cope with. And so they are unprepared.

The reality of death first hits most children when a favorite animal dies (although many do not have even this introduction to death in today's urbanized life). Or it may be a neighbor or a grandparent.

I think it is proper to speak of the reality of death, because the deaths children see on the screen (TV or movie) are only two-dimensional. The death of a public figure has more depth for children, but this is probably because they are sensitive to our own reactions.

When a barking, romping dog dies, though, a child sees what death is like. And he asks questions.

Why is he cold and stiff like that? Can I keep him in my room? Why do we have to bury him? Isn't it dark down there in the ground? What about when it snows? Does a dog go to heaven? Will I ever see him again?

Children need to be taught about death. They

cannot be forever sheltered from the reality, and so they should be prepared for it.

Our attitude is most important, and this is one big reason to explain death to a child when it seems distant, and the skies are bright, rather than when it is imminent or has already occurred.

Our attitude should be natural, matter-of-fact, positive. Everything that is alive (except God and perhaps His angels) will someday die. Death is the one experience in life that is shared by everybody. And it is shared by animals, too. Dogs and cats don't live as long as people; one day our dog will die.

For an animal, death is like going to sleep when you're really tired. Know how good bed feels sometimes? As far as we know, an animal never wakes up. We bury the animal in the ground to show our love for it, and because if we didn't, it would spoil and get flies on it and maybe spread disease.

But a person is different. A person goes to sleep, too, when he dies, but he wakes up afterward. And if he loves God, he wakes up in a wonderful place called heaven. This is God's special home, though God is everywhere.

I believe that our teaching about death should be coupled with teaching about heaven, that the emphasis should be on transition rather than cessation. The Bible explains heaven in terms of rest; this may be appealing to an older person, but hardly to a child. The child will respond to the other Biblical descriptions of heaven as a happy place, a beautiful place, a place of activity where there will never be sadness or tears.

When a person dies, his spirit leaves his body, in which it has always lived. A spirit is the real person, the part of us that nobody can see, the part that doesn't die. It's the inside you that says "God, I love you," when you don't even move your lips; that makes you glad when you obey and unhappy when you don't; maybe it's the part of you that remembers, that dreams happy dreams, that feels warm and cozy when you're sitting on mother's lap.

A friend of mine was forced to leave inland China with his wife and small children when the Communists took over the country in 1949. Each night of their flight to the coast they slept in a different peasant hut.

One night his wife died quite suddenly and unexpectedly. When morning came, he had to explain to his children that their mother had died, and also —seemingly most difficult for children to understand—that they would have to leave their mother's body behind, buried in the ground, and continue their flight.

"If ever I prayed for wisdom, for the right words, it was then. And God gave them to me. I reminded the children that we had stayed in different huts, and when morning came, the time to leave, we went on, leaving the hut behind.

"Mother's body was the house in which she lived, I explained. During the night, God told her to come home. So she went, leaving the house, in which she'd been staying, behind. That house was her body, and we loved it, but Mother no longer lived in it. So we would leave it there and put it in the ground when we left in a few hours. Somehow they accepted that simple explanation."

The simple explanation was also the true one. And when we explain death to children, we'd better be careful to stick to the facts.

He could have added, and doubtless later did, that God loves Mother's body, too—not just her spirit—and some day will perform the miracle of resurrection. Then He will make her body more alive than it ever was and reunite it with Mother's spirit—just as He did for our Lord Jesus on Easter morning.

When we talk to children about death, we shouldn't tell them anything that's not true. Maybe we'll feel that it's best not to answer certain questions at the child's age; if so we should just say that we'll explain more when he gets older.

As with teaching about sex, we must be careful not to force-feed, not to go beyond the immediate area of interest or attention. We should try to see things from the child's viewpoint and not impose our more sophisticated problems on his thinking.

Occasionally we are confronted with the necessity of telling the whole story at once, like my friend in China. It may be when a brother or sister or parent dies. Then we pray for special wisdom, for God to turn mystery and loss into beauty and hope rather than darkness and despair.

Explaining death to a child who himself faces it is an exquisitely painful task. On this I cannot generalize; I can only emphasize what seems to me the supreme importance of being truthful, and suggest that if you are ever confronted with this tragedy, you consult your doctor and pastor or other religious advisor.

But the child is yours, and the ultimate responsibility for handling the problem rests with you.

It is no small problem when your heart is breaking.

This possibility, remote though it may be, is a strong reason for giving our children religious training, for raising them in a climate of faith.

What are a child's impressions of death? We had a partial answer to the question after our 18-year-old son died, and we discovered a diary he had kept at the age of eleven, when his five-year-old brother died.

"About 2 p.m., something told me to pray for Danny. When I got home from school, I discovered that he had died just then! Debbie and I went up to the bedroom and saw him. We went and looked at a burial ground for four of the family. After we all ate (Daddy arranged for the funeral), a lot of people came over and we read the Bible, sang and prayed."

Two days later his diary entry was this: "Today we had Danny's funeral. There were a lot of flowers. The coffin was white. The service was a blessing. Then we went to see the grave. It was very unhappy, but Danny is with God. After we got home, Jerry Sterrett and I played ball in the yard."

12. When a Child Dies

OF ALL DEATHS, that of a child is most unnatural and hardest to bear.

In Carl Jung's words, it is "a period placed before the end of the sentence," sometimes when the sentence has hardly begun.

We expect the old to die. The separation is always difficult, but it comes as no surprise.

But the child, the youth? Life lies ahead, with its beauty, its wonder, its potential. Death is a cruel thief when it strikes down the young.

The suffering that usually precedes death is another reason childhood death is so hard for parents to bear. Children were made for fun and laughter, for sunshine, not for pain. And they have a child's heightened consciousness rather than the ability to cope with suffering that comes with maturity. They also lack the "kind amnesia of senility."

In a way that is different from any other human relationship, a child is bone of his parents' bone, flesh of their flesh. When a child dies, part of the parents is buried.

I remember a fish dealer on Michigan's Upper Peninsula telling me, "My brother died when we were kids. My father used to say that his son's death was something he'd bear his life long." (We were discussing the death of a Coast Guard officer's little boy, who had fallen overboard from the Mackinac Island ferry.)

I met a man who was in his seventies. During our first ten minutes together, he brought the faded photograph of a child out of his wallet—his child, who had died almost fifty years before.

The reaction of Charles A. Lindbergh to his infant son's kidnapping and murder, while it cannot be separated from his revulsion at the publicity and sideshow nature of the subsequent trial, is no surprise to anyone who has lost a child by death.

We have lost three: one at eighteen days, after surgery; another at five years, with leukemia; the third at eighteen years, after a sledding accident complicated by mild hemophilia.

I hasten to add that parents are not the only ones deeply affected by the death of a child; this death has profound effect on other children in the family, and on grandparents.

"It's like something is pinned to the front of your mind all the time," was our eight-year-old daughter's comment when her younger brother was in the hospital.

A common reaction to a child's sickness, especially if it is really serious, is for parents to question, "How did we sin? Why is our child suffering in this way?" When this happens, the parents' pain may become intolerable, complicated as it is by guilt.

Jesus Christ was asked this question by his disciples on one occasion: "Who sinned, this man or his parents, that he was born blind?"

His answer: "Neither this man nor his parents sinned. His condition is simply the occasion for a work of God to be done in him."

I do not mean to imply that parents of children who are born with a hereditary condition, or become sick, or have an accident, and die, are not sinners along with the rest of the human race. We are. Nor do I discourage self-examination and trusting God for forgiveness. We should.

But self-blame may easily lead to depression, and blaming husband or wife may lead to the breakdown of communication and distance in a relationship at the very time it is desperately important to parents, to the sick child, and to other children in the family.

Independent of everything else, of all other factors, the fatal sickness or accident of a child is simply the occasion for God to do a certain work in him. That work is to take the child home to heaven.

My mother put it this way: "If Jesus were here on earth and told you, 'I'd like Danny to be with me; I want to take over his teaching and his training,' you'd gladly give him up. And He's done that, by taking Danny to heaven."

We don't own our children; we hold them in trust for God, who gave them to us. The eighteen or twenty years of provision and oversight and training that we normally have, represent our fulfillment of that trust.

But God may relieve us of the trust at any time, and take our child home to His home.

The atmosphere of a home is extremely important if a child has a fatal disease. And parents, not children, determine that atmosphere. This is the time to be natural (impossible though it may seem), to trust God and let the children see that you're trusting Him. As much as possible, life should be lived as usual, without a lot of special gifts, Christmas in August, or a trip to Disneyland.

To spoil a child at a time of serious illness is to do him no favor. Few things are more liable to give away the fact that we are uptight about him than special treatment to a child. This is the time for treatment as usual, including—hard as it may be —necessary discipline. Of course we will spend more time with the sick child.

A pattern of obedience is a great help to a child who has or may-soon have pain; who must have shots and transfusions and other procedures; and who may have to be hospitalized, and adjust to a routine that he doesn't command.

The security of an orderly life, warmth and love, are what the sick child needs—and so do the well children in the family.

It's easy to forget that we have other children when we're trying to cope with the management of a child's pain and our own grief. And usually the other children understand the situation and make fewer demands on their parents.

But they need more, not less love at such a time. So do the parents.

A husband and wife who have been under the traumatic pressures of a child's terminal illness may find their own relationship severely strained, even deteriorating, weeks and months after the child has died. This is also true of a child's sudden accidental death.

The pattern is usually not the same for both parents, but it is basically one of withdrawal: not mentioning the child who died; breakdown of communication; escape into sleep, reading the Bible or other devotional books, and praying; pulling apart from one another in friendships, especially new ones; absorption in club or church activities.

At the very time that the other children need affection and warmth and love, their parents may be remote. Sometimes the children are left to fend for themselves emotionally while their mother spends long periods alone, reading the Bible or crying. And the father may find excuses to work late or spend time away from home.

This is the time to close ranks, the time for concern about your partner's affectional and sexual satisfaction, the time to force yourselves to talk to each other and to listen, and just to sit quietly together, as if your marriage depended on it. Sometimes it does.

Your other children desperately need your affection, after a brother or sister has died. But it is the overflow of your love for each other that they need, making the home a warm body of love, rather than showered affection from a husband and wife who have pulled apart from each other, and find compensation in their children. This may be emotionally damaging to a child.

The time after a child's death is when the family should do things together. Healing comes through family walks and games, a fire in the fireplace, meals out, special surprises. (And forget about all the meetings for a while.)

If it can be arranged, a family vacation trip after the child's death can be a most helpful influence in the family's restoration and healing. The trip should not be immediate, but several months later, when the initial shock has been absorbed and the long haul lies ahead.

It is easy to feel guilty about such a trip, or other happy family times after a child has died. It is easy and it is natural. Only the assurance that the child who died has entered into life beyond any life we can experience, and happiness beyond our trips, can free us from such guilt. For the sake of other children in the family, as well as ourselves, we should come to the point where we can say, "Wouldn't Danny enjoy this? I wish he were along with us."

Most of us keep our feelings to ourselves, even in our family. Openness to mention the problems and doubts, as well as memories of the child who died, and to discuss death, is an emotionally healthy climate for a home. Children—and parents —desperately need such a climate in death's aftermath.

It is our responsibility to create it.

A psychiatrist friend of mine says that we don't need to worry about trying to solve the problems and fears. Just provide situations in which the children feel free to express how they feel.

We've found that he's right.

13. Suicide

THE SADDEST duty of my life was to accompany a mother and father on their trip to a university in the mountains of Pennsylvania, to claim the personal effects of their son. It was Thanksgiving Sunday; the young man had jumped out of an eighth story dormitory window two nights before and killed himself.

I remember the words spoken by the dean of students to those parents: "We'd like to know what's going on in every student's mind, but with twenty thousand students, it just isn't possible."

Suicide is unusually difficult for survivors to cope with because it is avoidable. "Corellius Rufus has died," wrote Pliny the Younger two millennia ago, "and died by his own wish, which makes me even sadder; for death is most tragic when it is not due to fate or natural causes. When we see men die of disease, at least we can find consolation in the knowledge that it is inevitable, but when their end is self-sought, our grief is inconsolable because we feel that their lives could have been long."

What are the reasons for suicide?

Ill health, including pain; disappointment in love, loneliness, marital troubles; remorse, shame; professional or business failure; financial problems; disgrace, "loss of face." Sometimes these causes occur in combination.

Since suicide involves a decision of the will, it is questionable whether the act of a person who is mentally incompetent or psychotic, in taking his life, should be considered such.

In recent years, the suicide rate among young adults has been rising. The figures for 1969 compiled by the Los Angeles Suicide Prevention Center show a dramatic increase among people in the 20 to 29 age group, who had a higher rate than people in the 55 to 75, or even the over-75 age groups.

Among adolescents, the rate has also been rising. The struggle to achieve identity, blurring of sex roles, the fight for independence, difficulties at school, and contagion of suicide attempts are among the causes. The trigger may seem rather trivial from an adult standpoint: breakup with a boyfriend or girl friend, quarrel with a parent, for instance.

"The majority of adolescents who attempt suicide do not give those people around them any signals in the form of recognizable changes in behavior that the event is forthcoming," according to Drs. S. M. Finch and E. O. Poznanski. "Efforts to delineate a presuicidal syndrome in terms of behavior changes in the preceding three months prior to a suicide attempt have met with failure, except in those youngsters who are psychotic." (*Adolescent Suicide*)

André Haim suggests that there is a basic difference between adolescent suicide and adult suicide. Perhaps the real cause of suicide among the young is to be found in their being adolescent: the age itself may be characterized by a desire for death and a natural tendency to seek it. (Risk-taking in cars and cycles is high at this age.) And the adolescent has a tendency to overstep the boundary between a thought and its execution.

Alfred Alvarez speaks of "the two most sturdy fallacies [about suicide]: that those who threaten to kill themselves never do; that those who have attempted once never try again. Both beliefs are false. Stengel estimates that seventy-five percent of successful and would-be suicides give clear [verbal] warning of their intentions beforehand, and are often driven to the act because their warnings are ignored or brushed aside, or, like Mayakovsky's, treated as mere bravado. At a certain point of despair a man will kill himself in order to show he is serious. It is also estimated that a person who has once been to the brink is three times more likely to go there again than someone who has not. Suicide is like diving off a high board: the first time is the worst." (*The Savage God*)

Overwhelming guilt is often the reaction of the family and friends of one who has taken his own life. If ordinary death produces guilt over lost opportunities to be kind, to intervene in loneliness, to show affection, how much more this particular death.

Supportive friends, friends who are kind and available, are to a great degree the key to healing this grievous wound. But the survivor must also discover the secret of committing the past to God, to find forgiveness (for real or imagined guilt) from God.

The Mosaic law commanded, "Thou shalt not kill." This includes killing oneself, although the Bible does not single suicide out for special discussion.

There are five instances of suicide in the Bible. All were mature adults, most were outstanding leaders. The best known is Judas Iscariot, who hanged himself in remorse for betraying Jesus.

The examples indicate that suicide is not the will of God, even if our own experience did not.

But there is no Biblical parallel to adolescent suicide, to my young friend's leap from a high dormitory window.

At one time the church taught that suicide was the greatest sin, greater even than murder. The reason: there is no opportunity to repent afterward. (But how long does it take to repent and ask for God's forgiveness?)

The Bible does not contain a hierarchy of sins. And all sin, including suicide, is included in the forgiving work of Jesus Christ.

Can a mind break under pressure, like an arm or leg? I believe it can, and I believe that God "knows our frame, remembers that we are dust." This does not condone suicide; it does commit the person who takes his own life to God rather than to man's judgment. And thank God, He knows all the factors in the total situation.

14. Respecting Privacy in Death

EVERY GENERATION loses its leaders by death; they share mortality with ordinary men.

Lord Moran's account of Winston Churchill's final years was not unlike a doctor's record of the physical and mental deterioration of people we have known.

When a leader dies, a nation weeps. The stock market feels the shock waves. We are all affected.

But the tragedy of a leader's death may have helpful side-effects.

Our death-denying nation was suddenly confronted by death, in a form that resisted denial, when President John F. Kennedy, Senator Robert F. Kennedy, and Dr. Martin Luther King, Jr. were assassinated.

Common grief overcame the nation and the world. We were all forced to consider death and discuss it with our children.

I walked past the bier of General Douglas MacArthur, when his body lay in state in the Capitol rotunda in Washington. My impression was an overwhelming one of death's solemn dignity, and the greatness of leadership.

But a leader's death also poses serious problems, especially for his family.

One penalty of leadership is public exposure.

75

Billy Graham's biographers tell us of the difficulty he experiences in doing ordinary things with his family that the rest of us take for granted: dining out, taking a day off, even going on a trip by car.

Well-meaning, ordinarily considerate people rule out such occasions by intruding upon the leader's privacy.

For the leader, even sickness cannot be private. Former President Dwight D. Eisenhower learned that, and so did Lyndon B. Johnson.

And death becomes a public occasion. Children, parents, wives are on display on television and in the other media. Grief cannot be private.

But the privacy of sickness and death may be impossible for lesser leaders than those I have mentioned.

Recently I lost a friend, at least for a while, who died of cancer. He was not a world figure, but he had a lot of friends throughout the world. He was a leader for God.

Six months or so before he died, when his condition had just been diagnosed, a wave of disbelief and shock passed over the thousands of people who knew him. He was not yet old, he was physically strong and virile, he had a lovely wife and children, he had done great things for God and had established a fast pace in the work he was then doing.

Now cancer, which seemed to be the sentence of death.

If my friend had been an ordinary Christian, just as godly but not a leader, an ordinary church member, he and his family would have experienced the usual amount of Christian love and supportive prayer. His pastor would have talked with him, read the Bible, and prayed with him. He would have been remembered quite faithfully in prayer meeting. So would his wife and children. Food would have been brought in and other deeds of loving concern performed.

Perhaps—if my friend had not been a leader—some friends would have prayed for his healing in a simple, private manner. But the general attitude would probably have been one of acceptance: "God's ways are hard to understand, but we know that He will take care of the total situation."

Not so for the leader.

The privacy of suffering was denied him by well-meaning people near and far.

Surely God could not be taking this one home—what of the work he was doing? Think of such a life, nipped in the flowering. It could not be.

Then someone, perhaps a number of people, had the assurance that God was going to heal my friend. They had the assurance, and they shared it with him. All over the world, people prayed. And they wrote that they were praying, in most instances for healing.

The months of attrition and suffering became public. In a sense, God was being tested in such an important person's encounter with a malignant disease.

What could have been, for the ordinary person, a quiet dissolution of the bonds of life, a time of preparing to meet God—blessed, anticipated meeting—was denied my friend. And the intimacy of his impending departure was denied his family.

This is just my interpretation of this particular case of a leader who became sick and died. I have no reason to think that his personal reaction, or that of his wife and children, was anything other than deep appreciation of the concern shown by multitudes of people everywhere.

But I have known and observed other leaders in similar situations. The leader may be the pastor of a church rather than a world figure. But the effect of serious sickness is the same. Everybody gets into the act. Terminal sicknesses are no longer private.

What conclusions do I draw? Tentative ones, at best. But here they are.

The primary spiritual ministry to the leader and his family should come from the local group of Christians with whom they have been having primary fellowship in previous years.

Privacy should be respected. The person who writes a letter, makes a phone call, arranges something special, should ask himself: If I were in the spot the sick leader is in, would I want this done . . . perhaps by a hundred or a thousand different people?

We should recognize that God takes His leaders home at various ages, just like everyone else. He is showing just as good judgment when He calls such a person as when He calls the simplest, most inconspicuous person.

Whether the person is a leader or not, second-hand assurance that he will be healed—"God has told me, and I want you to know"—has no place in a Christian ministry to the sick. If the sick person and his family know God, He can speak to them. He needs no intermediaries.

The scope of praying by thousands of people, all over the world, for a sick leader's healing may subtly convince us that God will surely hear. Several Christians, praying for the ordinary church member, have little leverage; multiply it by several thousand, though, and the power of prayer seems obvious. But "if two of you shall agree," not two million, is our Lord's promise.

We can pray for people without letting them know we're praying for them. "Lord, give him strength to face today. Quiet his wife's fears for the future. Help the children understand that You are a Loving Father." Or "Please heal him, Lord. I know You can and I pray You will." God hears such prayers, even though the leader and his family don't know you're praying them.

I hesitate to mention this, but the glory of a leader's homegoing may be clouded by the confusion of people who believe God is healing him, right up to the finish line.

Death for the Christian should be a shout of triumph, through sorrow and tears, bringing glory to God—not a confused misunderstanding of the will of God to heal.

At the moment I write this, I have two other friends who have been told that they have malignant diseases. They are wonderful men and strong Christians. But they are not leaders widely known.

To be with them is a benediction. The crowd hasn't come between them and God.

15. Prayer and Terminal Illness

MOST CHRISTIANS believe that God has power to intervene in any illness, bringing healing. The miracles of Jesus Christ are examples of such intervention up to and including death, funeral procession, and the grave itself.

St. James advised the sick to seek healing, and prescribed the means: "Is any among you sick? Let him call for the elders of the church, and let them pray over him, anointing him with oil in the name of the Lord; and the prayer of faith will save the sick man, and the Lord will raise him up; and if he has committed sins, he will be forgiven. Therefore confess your sins to one another and pray for one another that you may be healed." (RSV)

The healing movements of recent years within most denominations and other groups find their basic authority in this New Testament passage.

Is the promise absolute, committing God to heal every sickness for which His intervention is sought in conformity with the terms of this passage?

Yes, say some, adding that lack of faith is the only obstacle that can block God's healing activity. And so, when prayer for healing is made, complete conviction that God has healed must follow. The burden of conviction is usually placed on the sick person, although others may bear it for him. Any doubt is banished from the mind, usually by the use of Bible passages related to prayer's efficacy and God's power.

Others believe that the promise of healing is not absolute, but conditional. The condition is God's sovereign will. Every request of man to God, they say, must have the essential element of Jesus Christ's prayer in Gethsemane, expressed or implied: "My Father, if it be possible, let this cup pass from me; nevertheless, not as I will, but as thou wilt."

According to those who hold the first-mentioned view, this sort of praying is self-defeating, since it implies doubt. For doubt is the enemy of faith.

But Jesus responded positively to at least one request for healing that involved an honest admission of doubt. "All things are possible to him who believes," He said to a man who had brought his boy for healing. "I believe; help my unbelief!" the father replied. And Jesus healed the boy.

The two views cannot be brought into accord in the limited space of this chapter, nor—probably—in any book, since both positions have been held for many years in the church without significant synthesis.

The problem that is relevant to a book of this nature is the effect of these views on the terminally ill patient and his family.

The Christian person who learns that he has a limited life expectancy is usually open to the suggestion that he pray for healing, or submit to the praying and ministrations of others.

He may be healed. Doubtless some have experienced divine intervention in what would otherwise be fatal conditions. (To be fair, we should add that some medical doctors point to spontaneous remissions, sometimes permanent, in incurable illnesses, which are unrelated to prayer for healing. Miracles today—as in the days of Jesus' life on earth—do not convince the person who excludes the supernatural. Such a person will not be convinced even if someone should rise from the dead, Jesus said.)

What are the effects of prayer for healing on a terminally ill person?

Tranquility usually follows, because God has been trusted to do what medical science admittedly is powerless to do. One important element of this sense of peace is usually a fresh experience of God's forgiveness and loving acceptance.

If close relatives of the ill person share his Christian convictions, a sense of God's control, of His love and oversight permeates family relationships. A hopeful attitude replaces the black curtain of despair that fell when medical sentence was pronounced. This "peace of God which passes all understanding" usually continues even though the person's condition may progressively deteriorate.

What happens if the prayer for healing is based on belief that God's promise to heal is unconditional, that lack of faith alone can circumvent healing?

If healing is not immediate and dramatic, depression may overtake the sick person. Normal discouragement over the physical condition may be heightened by a new dimension of self-blame and guilt for not having enough faith. Rarely does the sick person blame the "healer" or friends who are "standing with him" for healing.

He may decide that it is necessary to declare that he is healed, in spite of no evidence, or even of evidence to the contrary. If he is hesitant about committing himself in this way, friends may apply pressure, arguing that such a "stand" is necessary for God to heal.

This declaration of healing leads to unreality and death-denial in which husband or wife must share, or appear to share. So must other members of the family.

All relationships of the ill person are strained to a certain extent by this announcement of healing, relations with friends as well as with family. (Perhaps the closest parallel is the situation in which a well-meaning doctor tells a patient that he will get well, to keep up his morale, although his spouse and friends know differently.) As a result, life's final months are turned into play-acting instead of a mature, deepening experience with God and loved ones, based on a recognition of the possibility (if God does not heal) of separation by death.

Heaven recedes as a symbol of hope, and the man of faith looks to continuation of life on earth as the zenith of his desire no less than does the man of no faith. Death becomes faith's defeat instead of heaven's door.

The fact that death does not immediately occur in various incurable conditions, but that a pattern of interspersed remission and fresh activity may continue for months and even years, has a particular influence on some praying for healing. Hopes are raised, then dampened—if not dashed—by a cycle that would be considered normal by medical doctors, but is considered evidence that God is answering prayer by those who pray for healing. This alternation of crisis and encouragement is not easy for all who are involved.

Children in the home are especially vulnerable in these situations. The assurance by parents that God has healed father, mother or sibling is accepted at face value. Suddenly everything is bright and happy again; life can return to normal.

And for a time it does. But if God has not healed, a terrible letdown may be on its way. Death in the home is the most difficult incident with which any child must cope; to be confronted at the same time with the problem of parents who either lied or were wrong, or with a God who did not have the power to turn death aside: this compounds the emotional stress. Of at least equal importance, a long-range negative attitude toward God and the value of prayer may be created by such an experience.

Not that all cases in which a person dies after declaring that he has been healed have these harmful results. Because God is gracious, He often prevents spiritual and emotional problems from developing in the wake of honest mistakes made in faith's pursuit of His glory.

In the New Testament, healing was immediate. (When Jesus cured the blind man of Bethsaida,

His miracle was in two stages, but healing was still accomplished on the same occasion that the request was made.) Neither Jesus nor the Apostles kept people hanging, in order to prove their faith. Nor did they ask them to make a verbal acknowledgment of healing in the face of no evidence, or contrary evidence, as a sign of faith.

The attitude of New Testament Christians toward impending death was acceptance, not prayer for deliverance. In the days before his execution by Herod, John the Baptist sent disciples to Jesus to certify that He was the Messiah, not to plead for God's intervention in John's release and stay of execution.

St. Paul declared his ambivalence over death or the continuation of life in his letter to Christians at Philippi: "It is my eager expectation and hope that I shall not be at all ashamed, but that with full courage now as always Christ will be honored in my body, whether by life or by death. For me to live is Christ, and to die is gain. If it is to be life in the flesh, that means fruitful labor for me. Yet which I shall choose I cannot tell. I am hard pressed between the two. My desire is to depart and be with Christ, for that is far better. But to remain in the flesh is more necessary on your account." (RSV)

On a later occasion, faced with imminent death, St. Paul wrote to a godly young pastor, Timothy. In the letter he did not ask Timothy to pray that he would live rather than be executed—"I am now ready to be offered, and the time of my departure is at hand," was his reassuring word. But he did ask

Timothy to bring his cloak, because winter was approaching, and books to read in the prison.

When Stephen was stoned, he did not pray, "Lord, keep me from dying so that I may continue to serve you." His prayer was rather, "Lord Jesus, receive my spirit." And kneeling down, he died.

These illustrations are all related to the imminent termination of life by violent means, through martyrdom. It may be objected by some that they do not apply to ordinary sickness and death. Yet if Satan attempts to thwart a ministry and shorten a life through sickness, his power and work are at least equally as evident in martyrdom. Attitudes then become comparable.

I do not mean to imply that prayer for prolonged life is wrong when a situation appears to be terminal. No indication of this sort is given in the words of St. James, quoted earlier in this chapter; the opposite seems to be true.

But if such praying obscures the reality of heaven and its joyful prospect for the person who is ill, making it appear that only in prolongation of life on earth may satisfaction be found, it is less than Christian.

A pattern for communicating conviction about divine healing and deliverance from death may be found in the Old Testament account of what Shadrach, Meshach and Abednego said when King Nebuchadnezzar sentenced them to be executed. "Our God whom we serve is able to deliver us from the burning fiery furnace; and he will deliver us out of your hand, O king. But if not, be it known to you, O king, that we will not serve your gods." (RSV)

"But if not . . ." Here is an admission that we are fallible, that we may be wrong in our conviction that God will heal and thereby postpone death. (Death is always merely postponed, even if—as for King Hezekiah, when he "turned his face to the wall and prayed"—for 15 years.)

What we declare in these words is that our faith is in God, not in healing. Whether we live or die does not affect our bedrock faith in Jesus Christ.

And death, not healing, is the great deliverance from all pain and suffering. Death delivers God's people from the hands of persecuting governments, from the ravages of disease, and from every evil affliction.

A friend of mine who died recently, had prayed for God to heal him. He was convinced that God had answered and healed; but after a brief remission, the illness returned with full, terrible force. This could have been a devastating blow. But his final months, after surgery and chemotherapy, were not lived under any cloud. Instead, he was quietly confident, radiant with Christian hope.

"I prayed for healing, and God healed me," he explained. "He didn't heal my body, but He healed my mind and my spirit. He healed me of fear, of resentment, of bitterness, of worry for my family. This is God's answer to my prayer."

And you knew he wasn't rationalizing.

There is always the danger that a person who is zealous for healing will try to take the place of God in other people's lives. One man stayed at the bedside of a dying Christian leader for many hours. While he was out of the room for a brief period, the leader died. He blamed his absence for the death.

A month or so after our five-year-old died of leukemia, the same man—a sincere, well-educated Christian—told me that our son need not have died, if we had only possessed faith.

"Do you really believe that?" I asked.

"Yes, I do," he replied.

"Do you believe it enough to pray that your own child will become sick with leukemia so that you can prove your faith?"

After a long silence, he replied, "No, I don't."

I do not object to such zealots when they are dealing with other adults. I do object to the traumatic effect they may have on children and teenagers.

The summer after our eighteen-year-old son died, our sixteen-year-old daughter was at a Christian camp. A visiting minister, in the presence and with the silent acquiescence of the camp director, told this grieving girl, "Your brother need not have died, if your parents had only had faith for his healing. It is not God's will for one to die before the age of sixty."

When our daughter told us this in a letter, I thought about one who died in His early thirties, one who loved children enough not to hurt them.

16. The Funeral Director

A LOT OF BOOKS have been written in recent years that tend to demean the funeral director's function in our society. We have been told that he wants maximum profit from his profession; so do book-writers and medical doctors.

My own experience with funeral directors has been quite different from the caricature in the books. I have found them sensitive men in a profession that will probably never be appreciated, because it serves in a context of grief and emotional stress.

The funeral director reminds us of death. Small wonder that we want to forget him when the hearse is empty.

But the funeral director is a man, with all the feelings and capacities of most human beings. More than other men, except for pastors or other religious advisors, and doctors in certain specialties, he lives with sorrow. He is usually able to help us in our moments of grief—moments when the burdens of decision weigh heaviest.

If caskets have become more ornate and expensive, if cemeteries have become more country-club-like, if services provided by the funeral director have become increasingly elaborate, it is because we have demanded these things.

A funeral can be as simple and inexpensive as the law allows and the decision-maker desires.

The law complicates death and burial today. We can no longer put together a pine box and bury a corpse on our own property, as our ancestors did.

If a person has died without having seen a doctor within a prescribed number of weeks prior to death, an autopsy to determine the cause of death is mandatory in many jurisdictions.

If burial is delayed more than twenty-four hours after death, embalming is usually required by law.

Cemetery rules that involve such things as concrete vaults and grave opening times are further complications with which a funeral director must cope on our behalf, and at our necessary expense.

Where law and rules end, we take over. And it is here that we have ourselves, not the funeral director, to blame for a show of affluence and ostentation.

Why do we do it?

What makes us, or so many of us, throw ordinary fiscal caution to the winds when we're planning the funeral of a close relative?

On the surface, we want to show our respect and affection for the one who has died. In our gift-oriented, materialistic society, this means spending as much money as possible.

Even if we feel that this makes little or no difference to the one who has died, there are the other relatives to consider, friends and neighbors. What will they think?

Economists speak of this motivation as conspicuous consumption.

A more subtle motivation in large expenditures of money for funerals is guilt. Most of us have not been as kind, as considerate and self-giving toward the one who died as we know we could have been or ought to have been.

We didn't take her for an automobile ride last Sunday. We didn't write often enough. We didn't give him that set of golf clubs for Christmas. We never got around to anything more than talk about a wonderful trip to Disneyland.

So now we make amends, or at least give our guilt its outlet, by means of elaborate and expensive funeral arrangements.

If living with ourselves becomes easier as a result, if we can find even partial release from our burden of grief and guilt, it is probably money well spent.

But let's not blame the funeral director.

The basic expenses of a funeral are usually part of a standard fee set by the funeral director. Removing the corpse from hospital or other place where death occurred to the funeral home, preparation of the body for burial, use of a room and other facilities and personnel for the viewing and funeral service: these are the same for all funerals. And the cost is usually the same.

When someone for whom you are responsible dies, you phone the funeral director and ask him to take the body to the funeral home. He will usually do this immediately, although an autopsy causes delay.

For obvious reasons, it is advisable to decide on the name of a funeral director before death occurs.

This is hardly the time to thumb through the Yellow Pages. In many instances the person who dies has expressed a preference about this choice, and about other matters related to the funeral arrangements.

Later in the day, after the body has been taken to the funeral home, you will go there to decide on arrangements and to give the funeral director information so that he can prepare the death certificate and, if you desire, obituary notice for the newspaper.

This is the important time to take a friend along, someone with sound judgment who is not overcome by grief. Your pastor or other spiritual leader may be willing to accompany you.

The funeral director will want to know when you would like to have the funeral service and burial. He will ask about relatives and friends coming from a distance: have you allowed enough time for their arrangements and travel?

How many people do you expect at the funeral? Do you want to use the facilities of the funeral home, or your church or meeting house?

Do you want to have a time, probably the evening before the funeral, for the body to be viewed?

You will need a hearse for the trip to the cemetery. (Although, when our infant died, the funeral director gently asked if we wanted to use his black station wagon. This seemed more simple and appropriate to us, and we agreed. It also saved us money, since—like many others—this funeral director did not own a hearse, but rented one.)

Some decisions involve additional expense, beyond the basic fee.

Will you be able to provide pallbearers? Do you want to ask relatives and friends to carry the casket from the funeral home to the hearse, from the hearse to the open grave? If not, you will be charged an additional fee for the men—often employees of another funeral director—who will be required for this service.

You will probably want to supply the clothing in which the body will be buried. Otherwise you will pay for this clothing.

The funeral director will explain what motor vehicles—usually one in addition to the hearse—he will provide for the trip to the cemetery. If you are willing to have your friends drive their own cars, there will be no additional expense.

If—as often happens in our mobile society today—burial is to be in another part of the country from where death occurred and the preparation of the body took place, the funeral director will explain the various options available to you. For trips of less than three hundred miles, a hearse at a certain cost per mile is probably best. For longer trips, plane or train may be better.

In such a situation, it will probably be necessary to secure a second funeral director in the place of burial to meet legal requirements and to make cemetery arrangements there. The charges for his services will be additional.

The funeral director will explain the cemetery costs: opening the grave; a concrete vault (in which the casket is placed and sealed—which prevents later settling of the earth—required by some cemeteries, optional in others); and additional services. The funeral director has no control over these costs, and you may be billed directly by the cemetery for them. Either the funeral director or the cemetery may supply the vault.

If you (or the one who died) own a lot, you should bring the deed to the funeral director. If the lot consists of more than one grave location, he will need to know which one is to be used for the present burial.

If you do not already own a cemetery lot, the funeral director can give you advice and help you decide about this. It will probably be necessary for you to visit the cemetery and choose a location.

When purchasing a cemetery lot, find out what the requirements and obligations of the cemetery company are. Does the deed provide for perpetual upkeep of the lot? Are memorial stones permitted? Are you permitted to plant flowers, leave containers? These may be important matters to you or someone else in your family in the future, and you should find out about them before you have purchased the lot.

The funeral director will ask whether you want the local newspaper notified and a death notice published. This represents an additional cost, but is the easiest way to let friends and associates know about the death and arrangements.

Is there any special information you want included in this notice—did the person who died belong to any particular organizations that should be mentioned, do you want contributions to be made in his memory to some philanthropy, medical research or church in lieu of flowers?

Will you want music at the funeral, beyond the recorded background music that the funeral home usually provides? An organist and soloist will be an additional expense.

Do you want the funeral director to give an honorarium to the pastor or other religious leader who takes the funeral service, including this expense in your bill? Or would you rather take care of this yourself directly?

At this point, after he has led you in these necessary decisions, the funeral director will explain the cost of various caskets. Or he may take you to a room where they are displayed, open to view, with a card that gives the cost of each.

This cost for the casket usually includes the total basic funeral fee (for removal and preparation of the body, provision of hearse and other vehicles, etc.).

For some people, a room full of caskets from which to choose is unnerving and emotionally difficult, following closely—as it does—the traumatic experience of death.

If this is the procedure followed by your funeral director, don't hesitate to ask him to describe the various types of caskets and their prices. Then, after you have narrowed your choices down to a certain range, ask your pastor or other friend to examine them and decide.

Cremation arrangements will be made by most

funeral directors. Some costs related to this are less than burial, but legal requirements and local custom must be fulfilled.

As a professional person, the funeral director will be ready to serve you both before and immediately after the funeral, as well as accepting full responsibility for the service. He will not expect payment of his bill until afterward, when insurance policies are paid or the estate is admitted to probate. You may want to settle this at an earlier date, but usually you will be under no pressure to do so, either from him or from a legal standpoint.

Pre-planning for death is one way of simplifying this whole procedure. Before the need arises, and while the possibility of death seems remote, you choose a funeral director and discuss arrangements with him, reaching decisions that may not be implemented for years. A cemetery lot may also be purchased in advance. This procedure greatly lessens difficult decision-making, in a context of grief, for the survivor when death occurs.

This is the funeral director's function, a dual one: he is the one who disposes of our human corpses in a legal, decent manner; and he creates for us, the survivors, a final memory that we may more easily live with.

17. Our Death Celebrations

WE HAVE few funeral customs today.

No black armbands (though some of us can remember them from the past), no opening a window or removing a roof tile to permit the spirit of the dead person to escape, no wailing or dirges or tolling bells, no sackcloth and ashes, no burial dance or taboo on the use of the dead person's name.

Other times, other cultures may have celebrated death's visitation in these ways, but not ours.

The viewing and the funeral are our sole concession to death. As a result, they must bear a heavy weight of grief-expression, death-affirmation and memorializing.

Some people have decided ideas about the sort of funeral they want. Their desires may range from no viewing and a closed casket to selecting hymns and other parts of the service, and the person they want to officiate.

These preferences should be written out and left in a place available to the person who must make arrangements. They should not be included in the will, which might not be examined until after the funeral. (This is also true of requests or permissions for such procedures as an autopsy; leaving one's eyes or other organs for research or transplant, one's body to a medical school; contribution to a church, research foundation or charity in lieu of flowers; etc.)

Of course, the surviving next-of-kin has the final say about most of these matters. But an expressed desire from the person who died usually has heavy weight.

Before unusual requests are made in connection with the viewing or funeral, or decisions are reached, some consideration should be given to the function of these ceremonies.

For some people, death-denial is terribly easy. They cannot face the fact of their close relative's death, and as a consequence they postpone their reactions of grief rather than experience them immediately.

This sort of postponement of reality is potentially damaging. For such a person, a viewing and open casket may be a step in restoration and healing, rather than cruelty.

It's hard to deny death when one is standing next to the casket for several hours' viewing. In addition, words of comfort and remembrance from those who attend viewing and funeral are a source of strength to most survivors.

On the other hand, if you don't want a viewing, the decision is in your hands. If you want the casket closed during the funeral service, this too is your right to decide.

If there is any trend today, it is in the direction of shorter funeral services and less eulogizing.

From a Christian standpoint, the funeral of one who in life trusted Jesus Christ is a great affirmation of hope. This does not mean that sorrow and its expression are inappropriate; a funeral without sorrow is the funeral of one who lived a life totally alone.

But that sorrow is hope-filled; it is over our own loss, which we feel most keenly. We have no sorrow over the condition of the one who died.

When he was in his final illness, Dwight L. Moody, nineteenth-century leader in the church, made this statement: "Soon you will read in the newspapers that Moody is dead. Don't you believe it, for I shall be more alive than I am now."

"More alive than now": that is what we celebrate in a Christian funeral.

Clergymen, along with medical doctors and funeral directors, are frequently called upon to share the burden of grief when a person dies.

They do not find this an easy part of their ministry. Unlike doctor or funeral director, the pastor has usually known the one who died; he understands in some depth the survivors' suffering and problems as they face the future. And his function does not cease with signing a death certificate or consigning the body to a vault; his supportive ministry to the grieving only begins then.

The funeral of one who has not been part of his church, perhaps of any church, may pose a different sort of problem for a clergyman. Unless the service is to be purely perfunctory (which has its own built-in problems), the pastor is to a certain degree involved in a struggle between comforting the grief-stricken and being true to his religious convictions in what he says at the funeral.

His struggle is mine as I write. I know that I

must explain death and what follows as Jesus Christ and the writers of the Bible explained it, but I am aware that for many readers the explanation will bring no comfort.

But it can bring comfort to all by the simple exercise of faith.

I also know that even for many Christians, there is a conflict in considering members of their families—in some instances, the nearest and dearest—who died without giving any evidence of faith.

We cannot change the condition of a person in the afterlife, according to Jesus Christ. But neither can we know absolutely that one who died did not exercise faith in the closing, private moments of his life.

We have an example of this in the Bible.

When Jesus Christ died, one of the two criminals crucified with Him rebuked the other for reviling Jesus: " 'Do you not fear God, since you are under the same sentence of condemnation? And we indeed justly; for we are receiving the due reward of our deeds; but this man has done nothing wrong.' And he said, 'Jesus, remember me when you come in your kingly power.' And he said to him, 'Truly, I say to you, today you will be with me in Paradise.' " (RSV)

This is the only account of a deathbed conversion in the Bible, but it has great force because it involves a man near the bottom of the moral scale, and it also involves Jesus Christ as the authority for his forgiveness and admission to heaven. And it involves a very simple, uneducated faith—in effect, simply crying out to the Lord Jesus for hope beyond the grave.

I have observed deathbed conversions on two occasions. One was a New Englander, a shipyard worker who had lived more than 70 years without faith in Christ, without more than occasional attendance at church.

One day he had the sudden, alarming symptoms which required an immediate operation. Quite a jolt for a man who had never been in a hospital before, but had worked at the yard up to the very day he was admitted.

Time was short, and his son—a Christian—knew it.

" 'I am the door, by me if any man enter in he shall be saved.' That's the Lord Jesus' promise, Dad."

"Son, I'm coming in." And he came.

During those next two weeks they often heard him repeat the words, "Everlasting life . . . everlasting life." And once he quietly said, "I'm not afraid."

So deathbed conversion is possible today, and this opens a door to the possibility that one who lived without giving any evidence of faith in Christ may have turned to Him in life's closing moments.

But I cannot blur the essential fact that Jesus Christ taught: Death is a watershed. He is the one way to eternity with God. The alternative is eternal separation from God. In life we decide our destiny at death.

And although it is possible to turn to Him at the

end, we shouldn't presume on the possibility: we may die suddenly in an accident, or (as is more likely) we may get further and further from God as we get older.

"I used to think that people who knew they were dying, especially old people, would really be concerned about God," an Ohio State medical student once said to me. "But no more. I've seen too many in my clinical work in the hospital who couldn't care less.

"We've got one old lady in the hospital now who knows she has only a few weeks, a month or so to live. If I knew that, I'd be cramming for my finals. But do you know what she does? Reads from a pile of love and screen magazines every waking moment."

Most of us become crystallized in our opinions and outlook as we get older. Even death may not move us to become interested in God. This may be one reason that the Old Testament writer of Ecclesiastes advises, "Remember . . . your Creator in the days of your youth, before the evil days come, and the years draw nigh, when you will say, 'I have no pleasure in them.' "

In Dr. John Beattie's words, "More often than not, the art of dying is acquired at the beginning of life rather than at the end."

18. "Why Would a Kind God . . . ?"

A LETTER posed the question for me. But the problem was already there, in my own experience, years before the letter came.

The woman wrote from a small town in the East: "On January 25th, 1973, in Memorial Hospital, John Riso, red-haired, laughing, tall, eighteen, tractor-driving, cow-scratching, flirtatious, shy, died after two and a half years of leukemia. After six weeks of a raging temperature, experimental drugs, bleeding, and an abscess in his rectum that became gangrenous, he died soft and gentle, finally, after six hours of violent death throes. His face so thin, his hair only a memory, a soft red fuzz, arms blue and green from shots and intravenous feeding, he looked like an old picture of a saint after his tortures were over. . . .

"Why would a kind God do what was done to John, or do such a thing to me? I am poor, have only second-hand furniture and clothing. The things of value were my husband and sons. All our lives we have struggled to make ends meet. How can I live with the memory of the agony he suffered. Part of the time he was in a coma, and he kept saying, 'Mama, help me. Mama, help me.' I couldn't, and it's killing me. I whispered in his ear, 'John, I love you so much.' " All of a sudden his arm came up stiffly and fell across my back, and very quietly he said, from some vast depth, 'Me too.' "

There's the question: "Why would a kind God do what was done to John, or do such a thing to me?" Who has not asked it in the hours and days of suffering, of watching one close to his heart suffer?

I find no easy answer. Nor, probably, do you.

But finding none, we are in good company. Old Testament Job was in the dark, too, when all his children died a violent death. And a great theologian (Charles Hodge) said that if anyone thinks he has a simple solution to the problem of suffering, he should hold an infant screaming with pain in his arms, and any simple solution will fly out the window.

But somehow we start with the fact, admitted by the woman who wrote to me, that God is kind. Strangely, we continue to believe in His kindness, in spite of evidence that would seem to lead to a contrary conclusion.

Moses once prayed, "Show me now thy ways, that I may know thee." And God answered, for the psalmist says, "He made known his ways to Moses, his acts to the people of Israel."

Many people, like the Israelis at the time of the Exodus, are only interested in the acts of God. But the ones who want an answer to the problem of suffering must get behind and beyond the acts of God, as Moses did, and discern His ways.

God is sovereign. This is where we begin to answer our question. Our peace is not in understanding everything that happens to us and our children, but in knowing that He is in control of sickness and health, and even death itself. We accept life's mysteries and sufferings unexplained because they are known to God, and we know Him. Of course we seek answers from the Bible and from experience, our own and that of others. But when no answer is forthcoming, we don't attempt to rationalize ("It could have been worse," "Look at how many people heard the gospel through the funeral service," or "Things are getting so bad on earth; think of what he's been spared by not growing up"). Reason, we believe, is a deceptively weak crutch for faith. Reason gropes in the dark for answers, while faith waits for God.

But we also believe that God is love. He is kind, "He does not lightly afflict the children of men." I cannot explain it, but my wife and I have never been more convinced of His love for us and our children than when we have turned from a fresh grave.

Jesus wept with the suffering sisters of Lazarus, who had died. He suffered anguish of soul the night before His execution; He cried, "My God, My God, why have you forsaken me?" on the cross. He shared our humanity, our grief, our pain. But He also taught that God is sovereign, and He was the personification of His love on earth.

Here is the mystery: the kind and sovereign God permits suffering and agony.

One thing we must remember is that this is not "the best of all possible worlds." It is a world in rebellion against the kind God, a world of evil and sin and pain. It is a world, as Jesus explained, where God's enemy is at work.

In such a world, it is easy to forget God, to live only to enjoy the banquet hall without thinking about the painful exit door. But God will not permit this; He interrupts the banquet with suffering. "God whispers to us in our pleasures," C. S. Lewis wrote, "speaks in our conscience, but shouts in our pain. Pain is God's megaphone to rouse a deaf world." (*The Problem of Pain*)

We believe that in this world of evil, God's primary work, for our children and for us, is not to shield us from suffering, but to conform us to the image of Jesus Christ. And like Him (mystery beyond comprehension), we also learn obedience through the things we suffer.

God intends life to be character-building, and to this end He brings His people, the people He loves, into suffering situations. This was true of Job, although he was in the dark the whole time of his agony. A Christian response to suffering is a powerful testimony to the reality of Christian faith.

Death will some day be destroyed, but it is still a most painful experience which all of us must face. Many religious people have idealistic views of death-bed rapture and are unprepared for this enemy's grim violence. God has not promised His children an easy death, or deathbed visions of glory (although sometimes He may give them). He has promised an open door beyond.

Helmut Thielicke, contemporary German theologian, gives the final word, the answer to those who see in such a death as that of the "tractor-driving, cow-scratching" young man absurdity or meaningless suffering. He writes a "letter to a soldier about death."

"I do not want to close this long letter, dear comrade and brother, without opening to you yet one last perspective. Luther says in similar situations that only he who inflicts the wounds and permits them is able also to heal them. No one else. Illusions about death cannot do this; neither can hushed silence on the subject. Even the atheistic method of easy dying effects no healing; it only teaches how to bleed to death without looking. It proclaims the demise of an impersonal collective entity, not the end of a human being who is wrenched from just such anonymity when he is called by his name to be God's possession. No, God alone can heal the wound because he is the one who has inflicted it. Only He can heal it whose love reveals to us—so painfully and yet with such joy and promise—'the infinite value of the human soul.' . . . I am one whose history with God cannot stop, since I am called by my name and I am the friend of Jesus. The Resurrected One is victorious and I stand within His sphere of power. Once more it is his 'alien' life with which I am in fellowship and which brings me through everything and receives me on the other side of the gloomy grave. It is not the intrinsic quality of my soul nor something supposedly immortal within me that brings me through.

No, it is this Wanderer who marches at my side as Lord and Brother and who can no more abandon me on the other side than he could let me out of his hand here on this side of the grave." (*Death and Life*)

19. Two Kinds of Death

THE BIBLE describes death in various ways. It is "being gathered to one's people," "taking down the tent," "sleeping with the fathers," "departure," "dissolution of one's earthly house," and "rest."

These descriptions are for the event of dying and what follows.

The Bible uses the same word, death, to describe man's spiritual condition. We are "dead in trespasses and sins" according to St. Paul. Death is a state of sin and darkness in which all men are alienated from God, the fountain of life and light.

Used in this sense, death represents God's judgment for our rebellion against Him—our refusal to admit that we are creatures responsible to the Creator—and for our sin. (But physical death is part of the judgment: God condemned the first man for his disobedience with these words, "You are dust, and to dust you shall return.")

At the time Jesus Christ was born, according to St. Luke, the world was sitting "in darkness and in the shadow of death." Jesus described His mission in this way: "I came that they may have life and have it abundantly." And He made a great claim for Himself, related to death: "I am the resurrection and the life; he who believes in me, though he die, yet shall he live."

By His own death on the cross for our sins, and by His resurrection, Jesus Christ has brought life to men who were dead in rebellious sin. This life is available to all who turn to Him and put their trust in Him.

Therefore when we begin the life of faith in Christ, St. Paul says that we "arise from the dead" and become "alive to God."

We will someday die, like everyone else, but the enemy has been conquered; we have no fear of God's judgment in the afterlife. For that judgment was already suffered by Jesus Christ in His own death "for our sins."

Death then becomes for us, in the words of King David, "the valley of the shadow." Beyond the valley is unending and unshadowed life with God.

One blustery Sunday afternoon in February, several years ago, I spoke at a service in a convalescent home near Chester, Pennsylvania. Men and women were in wheelchairs, some listened from their beds in adjoining rooms.

Several of the patients were in their nineties, one lady was almost a hundred. She was weeping before the service began; as I leaned over to speak to her, she whispered, "I'm afraid to die."

When I spoke, I asked a question: "If I could promise to take you from this home to a beautiful spring-like place where you would be forever free from all your aches and pains, where you could walk and even run, hear and see, and never have any more loneliness or sorrow ever again; but if I had to take you first through a dark tunnel to get you there: how many of you would want to go?"

My question was rhetorical, but almost all of those dear old people raised their hands.

"Death is that tunnel," I explained. "It is not to be feared if we trust Jesus, for He will take us through it to heaven."

Our experience of heaven, according to the Bible, will be in two stages: first, immediately after death, a purely spiritual existence; later, a reunion of body with spirit.

During the first stage, our bodies will return to dust in the grave, while our spirits—the non-material part of us that constitutes the essential person—will go to heaven to be with God. One reason for this conscious spiritual existence without a body may be to convince us once for all that we are more than body, that—like God Himself—we can find completeness and fulfillment in a purely spiritual state.

(Some Christians believe that this first stage does not involve continued conscious existence of spirit without body, but rather a period of rest without consciousness. This state of soul sleep, according to these Christians, continues until the resurrection. Although no large part of the Christian church has held this view of what happens immediately after death, it creates no great problem. If you have ever gone to bed exhausted after a full, busy day of work, you know that sleep is a wonderful prospect, and that there is no consciousness of the passage of time before morning's awakening.)

The second stage will occur at a future date, when our spirits will be united again with our bodies. Christianity is not dualistic—it does not teach that the spirit is good, the body evil. Instead it says that the body itself has dignity and worth, and will be raised from its place of rest in the last day, to be reunited with the spirit, as Jesus' body was raised. As Job put it in the Old Testament, even though "worms destroy this body, yet in my flesh shall I see God."

After His resurrection, Jesus Christ had a body that was somehow different from the one that had been lovingly taken from the cross and placed in a tomb by His friends. It was His body, recognizable, including nailprints in the hands; yet it possessed a glory beyond.

This reunion of the individual's spirit with the body he shed at death, reconstituted and glorified, will take place at the time of Jesus Christ's second coming to the world.

Many questions about death are shrouded in mystery in the Bible.

The Bible has nothing to say about the current search for reliable guidelines to determine when death has occurred. It knows nothing about organ transplants or other death-delaying medical procedures. It doesn't describe the kind of funeral customs we should follow.

What it does tell us, and tell us clearly, is that by the death of Jesus Christ on a cross, death itself has been conquered, its bitter sting has been removed, and in a day yet to be, it will be destroyed.

It is enough.

20. Beyond the Tunnel

IN RECENT YEARS, as knowledge of the death process has advanced through research, concern about heaven has receded.

This is partly the result of our affluent society. Slaves, not freemen, hungry men, not well-fed, the ignorant, not highly-educated find heaven a longed-for prospect.

It is also related to the explosion of scientific knowledge and technological breakthroughs. When men orbit the moon, or land on it, space becomes more real than heaven.

"Where is up?" some people ask. And the statement of the Bible and creeds of the church that Jesus Christ "ascended into heaven," is made to seem a quaint myth.

Heaven then becomes a mere extension of life on earth. Heart transplants excite us because they promise a longer life span. Death can be postponed.

Only when we examine the quality of life here and now do we question its long-range satisfaction. Nation to nation, group to group, man to man, and even within our private selves we find struggle, frustration and disappointment.

If heaven is only a longing for something better, a rejection of what is, then a hedonistic philosophy is equally valid, certainly more satisfying: "Let us eat, drink and be merry, for tomorrow we die."

I cannot prove the existence of heaven.

I accept its reality by faith, on the authority of Jesus Christ: "In my Father's house are many mansions; if it were not so, I would have told you. I go to prepare a place for you."

For that matter, if I were a twin in the womb, I doubt that I could prove the existence of earth to my mate. He would probably object that the idea of an earth beyond the womb was ridiculous, that the womb was the only earth we'd ever know.

If I tried to explain that earthlings live in a greatly expanded environment and breathe air, he would only be more skeptical. After all, a fetus lives in water; who could imagine its being able to live in a universe of air? To him such a transition would seem impossible.

It would take birth to prove the earth's existence to a fetus. A little pain, a dark tunnel, a gasp of air—and then the wide world! Green grass, laps, lakes, the ocean, horses (could a fetus imagine a horse?), rainbows, walking, running, surfing, ice-skating. With enough room that you don't have to shove, and a universe beyond.

What is heaven like?

For the tired, it is a place of rest. For the sorrowing, a place where "God shall wipe away all tears from their eyes; and there shall be no more death, neither sorrow, nor crying, neither shall there be any more pain." Or war or greed or evil of any kind.

For all it is a place of total happiness: "In Thy

presence is fulness of joy, at Thy right hand there are pleasures for evermore."

Will we recognize one another in heaven? Yes, our personal identity will be maintained. King David found comfort, when his infant son died, in this: "Can I bring him back again? I shall go to him, but he will not return to me." And when the centuries-dead Elijah and Moses appeared with Christ on the Mount of Transfiguration, their identity was apparent to the disciples.

Heaven is also a place of activity, of work (but without the curse of toil and sweat and barren ground), of sharing in the responsibility of divine government.

I sat with a friend recently in his hospital room. The diagnosis is terminal cancer. If death comes, it will interrupt a distinguished career as a leader in training young men to serve Jesus Christ.

"When we think of heaven," he said, "I don't think we give enough consideration to what we're told in Revelation, that 'His servants serve Him,' and that their service is 'day and night.' We talk too much about rest—our rest will be found in serving God."

In heaven we will be freed from our present fragmented intellectual knowledge, and see truth and beauty with greatly expanded vision. "Now I know in part; then I shall understand fully, even as I have been fully understood."

Heaven will be supremely beautiful. The Biblical descriptions include walls of precious stones, gates of pearl, streets of gold.

(My mother used to say that she didn't find any

particular attraction in golden streets. I had no answer for her until I read a comment by F. B. Meyer, that in heaven all earth's values are turned upside down. "What do we count most valuable on earth?" he asked. "Gold. Men live for gold, kill for it. But in heaven gold is so plentiful that they pave the streets with it instead of macadam.")

Here is a classic New Testament description of what lies ahead for God's people: "Then he showed me the river of the water of life, bright as crystal, flowing from the throne of God and of the Lamb through the middle of the street of the city; also, on either side of the river, the tree of life with its twelve kinds of fruit, yielding its fruit each month; and the leaves of the tree were for the healing of the nations. There shall no more be anything accursed, but the throne of God and of the Lamb shall be in it, and his servants shall worship him; they shall see his face, and his name shall be on their foreheads. And night shall be no more; they need no light of lamp or sun, for the Lord God will be their light, and they shall reign for ever and ever." (RSV)

But, someone says, how could I enjoy such a place? I'm not made for it.

Neither is the fetus made for earth until he goes through the tunnel.

Or, as C. S. Lewis said, a young child, on hearing that adults find enjoyment in sexual intercourse, might ask, "What do they do—eat chocolate while they're doing it?"

Is there another place?

Yes, but if the reality of heaven is questioned today, the reality of a place of eternal separation from God (hell, as it is usually called) is ignored.

I accept its reality by faith, on the authority of Jesus Christ: "I tell you, my friends, do not fear those who kill the body, and after that have no more that they can do. But I will warn you whom to fear: fear him who, after he has killed, has power to cast into hell; yes, I tell you, fear him!"

Jesus Christ described it as a place of "weeping and gnashing of teeth," of remembering the past with its lost opportunity to repent and turn to God, of the loss of those gifts men enjoyed on earth without a thought of their Source: "From him shall be taken even what he has."

Jesus Christ defined hell's reality in stronger language than any other person in the Bible.

But He also had compassion on the multitudes, wept over an unbelieving city, and defined His mission as coming not to condemn, but to bring life.

"For God so loved the world that he gave his only Son, that whoever believes in him shall not perish but have eternal life."

21. "Death Be Not Proud"

THE HEARSE has come and gone. The brief grave-side service is ended, a handful of symbolic dirt has been scattered, the mourners have left, the casket has been lowered, damp ground now covers it.

A slight mound of earth stands above the surrounding turf. Flowers in disarray are its small badge of beauty.

The workmen go off down the gravel road, dragging their shovels.

Soon it will be dark. The rain will come, and in a few months the snow, the bitter cold.

When he dies, I'll just have to cover him up with dirt and forget I ever had him.

Perhaps someone will visit the grave. Jesus' Mother and a few friends visited His grave.

Some people find comfort through such visits. They sit and think, perhaps pray. Others find no comfort, only greater grief, and so they stay away.

But God is there. He does not despise the decomposing body. It belongs to one whose spirit lives with Him in heaven. Perhaps He sends His angels to guard it until the day of resurrection, as they guarded Jesus' body.

Some day He'll raise it up. He'll raise that

body from the dust and unite it once again, part and parcel, indissolubly, with the spirit that made it live, that gave it consciousness and personhood from the womb.

You look like a rational person. How can you possibly believe that the death of a man, or a little boy, is any different from the death of an animal?

I once saw some workmen move a little cemetery full of graves to make way for a building. One man stood in a deep hole, held up a small zinc plate: "Jennie Stewart, Died 1908." And then some moldy wood, a little dirt, a blackened skull.

"That's all there is of Jennie," he said, and laughed a short laugh. Then he put her in a box and began to dig a foot or two away.

You look like a rational person. How can you possibly believe . . .

Believe that God will raise up Jennie at the last day, the day of resurrection? Raise her up from two different graves?

Raise up your little boy, my three sons? Raise up you and me?

Because God is God. Because He's promised to. But most of all, because He raised up Jesus Christ, His Son who died, from the grave.

> Death be not proud
> though some have called thee
> mighty and dreadful
> for thou art not so.
> For those whom thou thinkest
> thou dost overthrow
> die not, poor death,

nor yet canst thou kill me . . .
One short sleep past
we wake eternally
and death shall be no more.
Death, thou shalt die.

—*John Donne*

One Saturday morning in January, I saw the mail truck stop at our mailbox up on the road.

Without thinking, except that I wanted to get the mail, I ran out of the house and up to the road in my shirtsleeves. It was bitterly cold—the temperature was below zero—there was a brisk wind from the north, and the ground was covered with more than a foot of snow.

I opened the mailbox, pulled out the mail, and was about to make a dash for the house when I saw what was on the bottom, under the letters: a Burpee seed catalog.

On the front were bright zinnias. I turned it over. On the back were huge tomatoes.

For a few moments I was oblivious to the cold, delivered from it. I leafed through the catalog, tasting corn and cucumbers, smelling roses. I saw the freshly plowed earth, smelled it, let it run through my fingers.

For those brief moments, I was living in the springtime and summer, winter past.

Then the cold penetrated to my bones and I ran back to the house.

When the door was closed behind me, and I was getting warm again, I thought how my moments at the mailbox were like our experience as Christians.

We feel the cold, along with those who do not share our hope. The biting wind penetrates us as them.

F. Scott Fitzgerald, writer of the twenties, who coined the phrase, "the Jazz Age," spoke of the end that was "desolate and unkind, to turn the calendar at June and find December on the next leaf." We have had this same desolate feeling, many of us.

But in our cold times, we have a seed catalog. We open it and smell the promised spring, eternal spring. And the firstfruit that settles our hope is Jesus Christ, who was raised from death and cold earth to glory eternal.

Books for More Reading

Alvarez, A. *The Savage God* (Suicide). London, England: Weidenfeld and Nicolson, 1971.

Bayly, Joseph. *Psalms of My Life*. Wheaton, Illinois: Tyndale House Publishers, 1969.

Finch, S. M. and Poznanski, E. O., *Adolescent Suicide*. Springfield, Illinois: Charles C. Thomas, 1971.

Frankl, Viktor. *Man's Search for Meaning*, Boston, Massachusetts: Beacon, 1963.

Harris, Audrey. *Why Did He Die?* (Explaining death to a young child). Minneapolis, Minnesota: Lerner, 1965.

Howard, David M. *How Come, God?* (Reflections from the Book of Job). Philadelphia, Pennsylvania: A. J. Holman, 1972

Hunt, Gladys. *The Christian Way of Death*. Grand Rapids, Michigan: Zondervan, 1971.

Kübler-Ross, Elisabeth. *On Death and Dying*. New York, New York: Macmillan, 1969.

Lewis, C. S. *A Grief Observed*. New York, New York: Seabury, 1963.

——————. *The Problem of Pain*. New York, New York: Macmillan, 1943.

Rudolph, Erwin P. *Goodbye, My Son*. Grand Rapids, Michigan: Zondervan, 1971.

Thielicke, Helmut. *Death and Life*. Philadelphia, Pennsylvania: Fortress, 1970.